Twayne's United States Authors Series

Sylvia E. Bowman, *Editor*

INDIANA UNIVERSITY

Langston Hughes

LANGSTON HUGHES

By JAMES A. EMANUEL

The City College

of

The City University of New York

 **123**

Twayne Publishers, Inc.   ::   New York

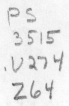
MANUFACTURED IN THE UNITED STATES OF AMERICA

To My Wife, Mattie Etha
AND
My Son, James, Jr.

Preface

THE LIFE AND WORKS of Langston Hughes have demonstrated his certainty about his function as a writer. "I try," he repeats, when asked about his writings, "to explain and illuminate the Negro condition in America." This volume, the first major study of Hughes, the first to attempt a literary examination of the writer's whole works, rather than a sociological glance at them, proposes to reveal how this senior Negro professional has brought clarity and beauty to his unusual variety of expressions. In an age of literary criticism still primitive in its attitude toward Negro artists, a close study of a versatile and authentic writer such as Hughes offers much to the mind and to the sensibilities. At a time when "the Negro condition" is fast becoming the American condition morally, it is vital that students—whose standard anthologies are significantly devoid of literature by Negroes—be offered an esthetic approach to the very substance which they will be required to transform by their future ethics and actions.

The chapters have been arranged to present, first, a comprehensive biographical and literary survey of Hughes to 1960, in order to provide a broad understanding of the author's main achievements in all genres, and of events and individuals that helped to mold his purposes. Subsequent chapters resort to analysis in depth of the most revealing works; these sections are thematically arranged, with concentration upon poems and short stories, the two forms which best illustrate his themes and variety of style. The final chapter fuses these approaches in a treatment of the author's productions of the 1960's, which establish important connections with his earlier genres and works in a way that shows the continuity of his purposes.

To read Hughes with sympathy and clear-sightedness opens doors to regions still dim to our perceptions. The function of literature, and our special need, is to awaken such awareness. The author's staple "dream deferred" theme adjures us to arouse our democratic selves. Perhaps this volume about Hughes will do a little to encourage acceptance of the challenge that has long outfaced "the academy": full exploration of Negro writers.

J. A. E.

The City College of New York
September 6, 1966

Acknowledgments

For a fellowship to complete this study, I am indebted to The Eugene F. Saxton Memorial Trust. Helpful cooperation came from the staffs in charge of the James Weldon Johnson Memorial Collection at Yale and the Schomburg Collection in Harlem, who made available voluminous material. I am grateful to my wife, Mattie Etha, for her sensitive reading of the manuscript as it grew. I extend particular appreciation to Mr. Hughes, who repeatedly opened his personal files, made my use of them comfortable, answered my many questions without any attempt to influence my judgments, and gave me permission to quote variously from his works.

For permission to quote from copyrighted material, acknowledgment is made to the following:

Alfred A. Knopf, Inc., for *The Weary Blues* (1926), *Fine Clothes to the Jew* (1927), *The Dream Keeper* (1932), *The Ways of White Folks* (1934), *Shakespeare in Harlem* (1942), *Fields of Wonder* (1947), *One-Way Ticket* (1949), *Selected Poems of Langston Hughes* (1959), and *Ask Your Mama* (1961).

Hill & Wang, Inc., for *The Big Sea* (1963), *Something in Common and Other Stories* (1963), and *I Wonder As I Wander* (1964).

Harold Ober Associates, Inc., for *Simple Stakes a Claim* (1957).

Simon & Schuster, Inc., for *Simple Speaks His Mind* (1950) and *Simple Takes a Wife* (1953).

Contents

Chronology

1902 James Langston Hughes born February 1 in Joplin, Missouri, to James Nathaniel and Carrie Mercer Langston Hughes.

1903- Lived in Buffalo; Cleveland; Lawrence, Kansas; Mexico
1914 City (where separation of father and son began, 1907-19); Topcka, Kansas; Colorado Springs; Lawrence again (with grandmother); Kansas City.

1915 Completed grammar school in Lincoln, Illinois; read first poem, written as class poet, at graduation.

1916- Attended Central High School in Cleveland; wrote first
1920 short story there. Spent depressing summer in Mexico with father in 1919.

1921- Taught school in Mexico. Published first prose piece,
1922 "Mexican Games," in *Brownie's Book*, "The Negro Speaks of Rivers" in *The Crisis*. Attended Columbia University.

1923- Read poems for first time publicly in New York. Worked
1924 on ships bound for Africa and Holland; employed in Paris night clubs; stranded as a beachcomber in Genoa.

1925 Lived in Washington, D. C. Began to meet principals of Harlem Renascence. Began to use blues and spirituals in poetry. Won poetry prizes in contests held by *Opportunity* and *The Crisis*. Sold for first time poems to *Vanity Fair*. Publicized as "bus boy poet."

1926 Sold stories to *Messenger*. Lived in summer by writing lyrics and sketches for musical revue. *The Weary Blues*.

1927 *Fine Clothes to the Jew*. Took first poetry-reading tour of South. Went South with Zora Hurston to find folklore materials. Read poems to musical accompaniment at Princeton University.

1929 Received B.A. from Lincoln University, Pennsylvania.

1930 *Not Without Laughter*. Worked with Zora Hurston on Negro folk comedy *Mule Bone*. Alienated from patron in December.

1931 Received Harmon Gold Award for Literature. *Dear Lovely Death* privately printed. Journeyed to Haiti, took first cross-country poetry-reading tour (aided by Rosenwald Fund Fellowship); went to Soviet Union with movie-making group.

1932 *The Dream Keeper.*

1934 *The Ways of White Folks.* Death of father in Mexico.

1935 Awarded Guggenheim Fellowship. Lived and wrote in Mexico, California, Ohio (where mother was ill in Oberlin), New York. Five-year-old *Mulatto* began successful Broadway run.

1936 Began to have several plays performed by Negro theatrical groups.

1937 Became correspondent reporting Civil War in Spain. Published "Letters from Spain" there in *Volunteer for Liberty* and *El Mono Azul.* Death of mother.

1938 Founded the Harlem Suitcase Theater.

1939 Founded The New Negro Theater in Los Angeles.

1940 *The Big Sea.* Wrote stories at Hollow Hills Farm near Monterey, California; aided by Rosenwald Fund Fellowship.

1942 *Shakespeare in Harlem.* Founded Skyloft Players in Chicago. Began five-year residence on St. Nicholas Ave. (Harlem).

1943 Began *Chicago Defender* "Simple" columns. Received Doctor of Letters degree from Lincoln University.

1944 *Lament for Dark Peoples and Other Poems* published anonymously by the anti-Nazi underground in Holland.

1946 Received grant from American Academy of Arts and Letters.

1947 Roumain's *Masters of the Dew,* translated with Mercer Cook. *Fields of Wonder.* Became poet-in-residence at Atlanta University. Settled permanently in his own home in Harlem.

1948 Nicolás Guillén's *Cuba Libre,* translated with Ben Frederic Carruthers.

1949 *The Poetry of the Negro, 1746-1949*, edited with Arna Bontemps. Taught at the Laboratory School, University of Chicago. *Troubled Island* (libretto by Hughes) presented in New York.

1950 *Simple Speaks His Mind. The Barrier* (libretto by Hughes) presented in New York and Ann Arbor.

1951 Federico García Lorca's *Romancero Gitano*, translated by Hughes, published by *Beloit Poetry Journal. Montage of a Dream Deferred.*

1952 *The First Book of Negroes. Laughing to Keep from Crying.*

1953 Received Anisfield-Wolfe Award. *Simple Takes a Wife.*

1954 *Famous American Negroes. First Book of Rhythms.*

1955 *The First Book of Jazz. Famous Negro Music Makers. The Sweet Flypaper of Life* (text by Hughes, photographs by Roy De Carava).

1956 *I Wonder As I Wander. A Pictorial History of the Negro in America,* with Milton Meltzer. *The First Book of the West Indies.*

1957 *Selected Poems of Gabriela Mistral,* translated by Hughes. *Simple Stakes a Claim. Simply Heavenly* presented on Broadway and in Hollywood.

1958 *The Langston Hughes Reader. Famous Negro Heroes of America. The Book of Negro Folklore,* edited with Arna Bontemps.

1959 *Tambourines to Glory. Selected Poems of Langston Hughes.*

1960 *The First Book of Africa. An African Treasury,* edited by Hughes. Received NAACP's Spingarn Medal. Was host on WABC-TV's "Expedition: New York" in December.

1961 *The Best of Simple. Ask Your Mama. Black Nativity* presented in New York. Elected to National Institute of Arts and Letters.

1962 *Fight for Freedom: The Story of the NAACP.* Attended literary conference in Uganda and Nigeria. Read at first National Poetry Festival at the Library of Congress. Began *New York Post* "Simple" columns.

1963 *Something in Common and Other Stories. Five Plays by Langston Hughes,* edited by Webster Smalley. *Poems from Black Africa. Tambourines to Glory* (play based on novel) presented on Broadway. Received Doctor of Letters degree from Howard University.

1964 *New Negro Poets: U.S.A.,* edited by Hughes. *Jerico-Jim Crow* presented in New York. Helped prepare BBC's "The Negro in America" autumn series.

1965 *Simple's Uncle Sam. The Prodigal Son* presented in New York. Wrote script for WCBS-TV's Easter program, "It's a Mighty World." Lectured in America Houses in Europe for United States Information Agency.

1966 *La Poésie Négro-Américaine,* edited by Hughes. *The Book of Negro Humor,* edited by Hughes.

1967 *The Best Short Stories by Negro Writers,* edited by Hughes. *The Panther and the Lash. Black Magic: A Pictorial History of the Negro in American Entertainment,* with Milton Meltzer.

Langston Hughes

CHAPTER 1

The Big Sea

Literature is a big sea full of many fish.
I let down my nets and pull.
                                        —*The Big Sea*

LANGSTON HUGHES opened his first volume of poems
with this expression of his—and every Negro's—"soul world":
"I am a Negro:/Black as the night is black,/Black like the
depths of my Africa." When the woman in the box office of the
only movie theater in Lawrence, Kansas, pushed the twelve-
year-old boy's nickel back and pointed to the new sign, "Colored
Not Admitted," she laid a shaping hand on that world. Hughes
has spent a lifetime illuminating it—through poems, stories,
novels, lectures, and various other literary forms—with a virtu-
osity and understanding so genuine that he has been unofficially
granted such titles as Negro Poet Laureate and Dean of Negro
Writers in America.

His life, which began in Joplin, Missouri, on February 1, 1902,
has been filled with adventure, diversity, and honors. Hughes
has crossed the United States many times, reading his poems on
hundreds of occasions. His reputation and friendships abroad
have been spread by world-wide travels: he has slept in a drain
pipe in Haiti, gone hungry with beachcombers in Genoa, and
lived among the Uzbeks of Samarkand. Many honors have
marked the life of this author who never has succumbed to the
blandishments of marriage or settled living. Literary prizes,
grants, fellowships, and other awards have appeared regularly
ever since 1925, when Hughes won the first poetry prize offered by the editors of *Opportunity* for "The Weary Blues"—and
spent his forty-dollar prize getting to the banquet to collect it.

I *Legacies of Color*

This auspicious career began—save for the year or so in the home that disintegrated as mother and father went separate ways—in the care of Hughes's proud maternal grandmother, Mary Sampson Patterson Leary Langston of Lawrence, Kansas.[1] Mrs. Langston, of Indian and French ancestry, had been free in ante-bellum North Carolina, had attended Oberlin College, and had married freeman Lewis Sheridan Leary. His legacy for her was a bloodstained, bullet-riddled shawl, sent back to her after John Brown's raid at Harper's Ferry; for there young Leary died in action, one of five Negroes known to have fought with Brown.[2] Her second husband, Hughes's grandfather, had been Charles Langston, a man active in the Oberlin station of the Underground Railway.

Hughes's paternal lineage reaches back to Francis Quarles, the seventeenth-century English poet; and it reputedly touches Henry Clay as brother of Sam Clay of Henry County, Kentucky, the paternal grandfather of James Nathaniel Hughes. The contempt of Langston's father for Negroes and poor people, his bitterness over prejudice that denied him a chance to take the examination for the bar in Oklahoma, and his disdain for all who tolerated discrimination pushed this little, rapidly striding, mustachioed man away from his Joplin family to Cuba and Mexico. James Nathaniel Hughes, who spent his remaining thirty years practicing law and improving his big ranch in the mountains beyond Toluca, ignored his son's ambitions.

Hughes's mother, who had a minor artistic bent, occasionally wrote poems, gave dramatic recitations, and read papers at the Inter-State Literary Society founded by Hughes's grandfather. She took her small son to plays in Topeka, Kansas. But her influence upon him was attenuated by her sporadic travels in search of better employment. Having studied at the University of Kansas, and being militant enough to win a fight against segregated schooling for her first-grader in Topeka, she was never content with menial jobs. The racial pride that deprived Hughes of a father was also responsible for taking away his mother.

These circumstances placed him, at the age of seven, in Lawrence, Kansas, in his grandmother's house on Alabama Street near the University. It was his home until her death in 1914, with the exception of occasional months with his mother and one brief trip to see his father in Mexico. Hughes's earliest memory that is important to his stories and poems—throwing light upon their usual lack of sentimentality—recaptures his grandmother, with Sheridan Leary's shawl (now a memento in the Ohio State Historical Museum) pulled across her shoulders:

> She sat, looking very much like an Indian . . . in her rocker and read the Bible, or held me on her lap and told . . . stories about people who wanted to make the Negroes free. . . .
> Through my grandmother's stories always life moved, moved heroically toward an end. Nobody ever cried. . . . They worked, or schemed, or fought. But no crying. When my grandmother died, I didn't cry either. [Her stories] taught me the uselessness of crying about anything.

The boy's not unusual method of escape from loneliness under the old woman's rather stern tutelage appears in another passage from *The Big Sea*, which recounts his first visit, at five, to a Topeka library: "There I first fell in love with librarians. . . . The silence . . . the big chairs, and long tables, and the fact that the library was always there and didn't seem to have a mortgage on it, or any sort of insecurity about it—all of that made me love it . . . so that after a while, . . . I believed in books more than in people. . . ." In the relieving books, he writes, "if people suffered, they suffered in beautiful language, not in monosyllables, as we did in Kansas."

After a year or more in the Lawrence home of his mother's friends, whom he called Uncle and Auntie Reed, Hughes, now fourteen, went to Lincoln, Illinois, to stay with his mother and stepfather, Homer Clark, and their son. Clark, a chef, often had to leave to search for a job. By 1916, the home seemed fatherless.

But Homer Clark beckoned from the steel mills of Cleveland, and Hughes graduated there from Central High School in 1920. His reading at school was important, and Hughes records examples of it in *The Big Sea*. The only poems he liked were Paul Laurence Dunbar's and Longfellow's *Hiawatha,* but he liked all kinds of stories. He read, among others, the novels of Edna Ferber, Harold Bell Wright, Zane Grey and Theodore Dreiser; he familiarized himself with works by Schopenhauer and Nietzsche. He was especially stirred by the prose of W. E. B. DuBois's *Souls of Black Folk* and by the beauty of

Maupassant's stories in French. Through his English teacher, Ethel Weimer (whose lessons on truth and beauty in unconventional art seem reflected in Hughes's insistence on "honest" writing), he became acquainted with the poetry of Carl Sandburg (whom he calls his "guiding star"), Amy Lowell, Vachel Lindsay, and Edgar Lee Masters.

II Susanna Jones and Mary Winosky

Hughes was becoming a writer, too. His earliest poem he wrote as class poet (and only Negro boy) of his Lincoln elementary school graduating class. In Cleveland, he wrote for the high school *The Monthly* and *Belfry Owl*, took an interest in playwriting, and edited the senior yearbook. During these years, Hughes carefully separated his "whole notebook full of poems" from "another one full of verses and jingles." Some of the poems show unquestionable merit. When only seventeen, he wrote a poem that, almost half a century later, was included in a television show, "Beyond the Blues," aimed at "the sophisticated mind and not the ethnic-conscious heart."[3] *The Crisis*, February, 1923, contains this poem, "When Sue Wears Red," about a chocolate-skinned girl from the South:

> When Susanna Jones wears red
> Her face is like an ancient cameo
> Turned brown by the ages.
>
> Come with a blast of trumpets,
> Jesus!
>
> When Susanna Jones wears red
> A queen from some time-dead Egyptian night
> Walks once again.
>
> Blow trumpets, Jesus!
>
> And the beauty of Susanna Jones in red
> Burns in my heart a love-fire sharp like pain.
>
> Sweet silver trumpets,
> Jesus!

Hughes had not heard jazz in the Grand Duc in Paris or walked down noisy Seventh Street in Washington, D. C., or searched folklore; yet he had absorbed the thrusting, fervent refrain that was to be one sign of his authenticity in a new kind of poetry. As a high-school boy of fourteen, he could imitate Dunbar by opening a poem with

> Just because I loves you—
> That's de reason why
> My soul is full of color
> Like de wings of a butterfly.

But it was not only Sandburg who led him to write, about the same time,

> The mills
> That grind and grind,
> That grind out steel
> And grind away the lives
> Of men—

for he saw the mills grind down his stepfather until light janitorial work was all that he could perform.

Young Hughes, whose purposes were quickly to outgrow the matter and techniques of Dunbar and Sandburg, was becoming a Negro poet. To be alive to the meaning of race in Hughes's career, one must consider ways in which his being a Negro had lodged in his consciousness by 1920. Racial prejudice not only impoverished his boyhood family life but had insidious effects. As a second-grader in Lawrence, he had been placed in a segregated room with Negro children from six different grades. In the seventh grade at Central School (after the rebuff at the movie theater), he had been placed in a separate row with the two other Negro pupils at the back of the room. Outside the classrooms, the small Negro populace discussed the editorials in *The Crisis,* the organ of the new National Association for the Advancement of Colored People, and engaged in the ideological controversy involving the conciliatory racial policies of Booker T. Washington and the militant dictums of W. E. B. DuBois.

The complexity of Hughes's environment is reflected by his first short story, "Mary Winosky," written in 1915 to fulfill a high-school English assignment, probably Ethel Weimer's.[4] Developing a newspaper item ("Mary Winosky, who scrubbed floors and picked rags, died and left $8,000"), Hughes employs narrative techniques characteristic of many later stories: atmospheric refrains, contrasting images, sentence fragments. Unsentimental, it shows his humanity as a writer, for some of his

experiences near the time of writing might have shored his imagination against the tragedy in a nondescript white girl's
scrub-bucket life.

Hughes was living with his mother, stepfather, and half brother
in a crowded attic or basement on Cleveland's east side, among
sheds, garages, and stores serving as family dwellings. Emerging
from among the newly migrated Southern Negroes who had to
pay double and triple rent for such makeshift quarters, the boy
went to a once aristocratic school then attended almost entirely
by immigrant students born in Poland, Hungary, Italy, Russia,
and elsewhere. He was a good student, popular as an athlete, and
a military training corps lieutenant. Some of his many class and
club offices he won as a Negro because of a Jewish-Gentile
deadlock.

"My best pal in high school was a Polish boy named Sartur
Andrzejewski," Hughes writes in *The Big Sea,* adding, "His rosy-
cheeked sisters were named Regina and Sabina." With such
friends he went to his first symphony concert; from them he
learned "that Europe was not so far away"; and about them he
learned "that lots of painful words can be flung at people" besides
those hurled at Negroes—besides those which had accompanied
stones and cans thrown at him in Lawrence by classmates spurred
on by a teacher's racial remarks. But he remained mindful of his
own heritage of color. In Chicago in 1918, Hughes records,
"South State Street was in its glory . . . a teeming Negro street.
. . ." And from beyond Wentworth Street, where the boy strayed
his first Sunday in town, a group of white boys returned him
to State Street with two black eyes and a swollen jaw..

This story forecasts Hughes's ability as a writer to withdraw
from, transcend, and thus merge his Negro- and white-oriented
experiences. Scrubwoman Mary Winosky apparently ate vinegar-
flavored cabbage like that he enjoyed at Sartur's home. But the
roaring elevated trains that replaced the Winoskys' expected
birdsongs just as likely echoed the ones that kept the author's
family restless during hot nights.

III *Misery and Poetry: from Mexico to Harlem*

By 1921, two important events occurred in Hughes's life. The
first, in August, 1919, in a season *The Big Sea* calls "the most
miserable I have ever known," was his discovery that he hated

his father. Feverish and yellow-eyed in the American Hospital in Mexico City, felled by a stomach-turning revulsion that doctors could not diagnose, Hughes faced the realization that would, within three years, end his relationship with his father. His twenty-dollar-a-day illness had been augured by a crisis surmounted in his father's empty house several weeks earlier: ". . . I put the pistol to my head and held it there, loaded, a long time. . . . I began to think, if I [shoot] I might miss something. I haven't been to the ranch yet, nor to the top of the volcano, nor to the bullfights in Mexico, nor graduated . . . nor got married. So I put the pistol down. . . ."

The other important event that occurred while he was in Mexico was the beginning of Hughes's career, although not until nine years later would he start living by his writings alone. He began publishing poetry—other than that printed by school-mates—in June, 1921, when "The Negro Speaks of Rivers" appeared in *The Crisis*. These two years or more comprise half of a span of poetry writing (from the summer of 1919 to the fall of 1923) unrivaled in Hughes's life for its continuity and quality of production.

Early in 1921 Hughes began to write prose in hopes of publication. He made unsatisfactory attempts to describe the bullfights he saw almost weekly. Not long before *The Crisis* printed "The Negro Speaks of Rivers," its editor accepted an article about Toluca, one about the Virgin of Guadalupe, and a children's play, *The Gold Piece*—all for the *Brownie's Book* just begun by DuBois. These acceptances marked the beginning of a long and charming literary correspondence with Jessie Fauset, then managing editor, who later was the author of four novels. Hughes writes in *The Big Sea* that for a few years after 1921 his poems "appeared often (and solely)" in *The Crisis*.

When he left Mexico in September, 1921, for Columbia University, Hughes could look back upon varied experiences south of the border. Behind him were horseback rides through mountains dotted with bandits (who had once divested his father, in a pine forest, of all but his underwear); the finishing school in which he had taught English; his enforced learning of German and Spanish—languages in which his father was brusquely eloquent, in contrast to his stubborn silence in English.

Hughes's academic year at Columbia was the start of an often thrilling period that ended in the spring of 1923. Bound there only as an alternative to heeding his father's demand that he attend European colleges to become an engineer in Mexico, he was motivated by an eagerness to see Harlem. When he emerged from the subway at 135th Street and Lenox Avenue, he wanted to shake hands with the hundreds of Negroes around him. *The Big Sea* covers his stay at Columbia in three pages: he did not like its bigness, his classmates and courses, or the discrimination he found at Hartley Hall and among the staff of the *Spectator*. He preferred to read on his own, attend lectures at the Rand School by Ludwig Lewisohn and Heywood Broun, or repeatedly see the revue *Shuffle Along*.

When Hughes wrote his father in the spring of 1922 that he was leaving Columbia to go to work, their correspondence ended. After laboring on a Staten Island truck-garden farm and later making deliveries for a Manhattan florist, Hughes took a job as mess boy on an old freighter. But the ship was bound nowhere. Towed up the Hudson to Jones Point, it lay all winter with about eighty other unseaworthy vessels. The seagoing author eased his disappointment by reading the ship's library, that included Samuel Butler's *The Way of All Flesh*, Gabriel d'Annunzio's *The Flame of Life,* and Joseph Conrad's *Heart of Darkness*.

Although Hughes records that he wrote many poems that winter, he does not name any of them except "The Weary Blues," written about a piano player he had heard in Harlem. The poem appeared in New York's *Amsterdam News,* a Negro newspaper, on April 8, 1923. By that spring, *The Crisis* had published several poems of substantial merit: "The Negro," "To a Dead Friend," "Danse Africaine," "Song for a Banjo Dance," "The South," "Mother to Son," and "When Sue Wears Red." Lesser but effective poems had been printed during the same period, some in spring numbers of Columbia's *Spectator*. Hughes's reputation was growing. *The Crisis* staff invited him to luncheon, and Alain Locke of Howard University made a futile attempt to get an invitation to speak with the shy poet at Jones Point.

IV   "I threw the books in the sea": Africa, Paris, and Italy

When spring moved Hughes to search for an ocean-going ship, he found the S.S. *Malone,* bound for Africa. Eager for six

months of new experiences, he wanted on the night of departure
to purge his system of books. Standing topside off Sandy Hook,
he looked at the box of them he had just retrieved from his
Harlem landlady, Mrs. Dorsey. He thought:

> . . . they seemed too much like everything I had known in the
> past, like the attics and basements in Cleveland, like the lonely
> nights in Toluca, like the dormitory at Columbia, like the fur-
> nished room in Harlem, like too much reading all the time when
> I was a kid, like life isn't, as described in romantic prose;
> . . . it wasn't only the books that I wanted to throw away, but
> everything unpleasant . . . the memory of my father, the poverty
> and uncertainties of my mother's life, the stupidities of color-
> prejudice, . . . the fear of not finding a job, the bewilderment
> of no one to talk to about things that trouble you, . . . I wanted
> to be a man on my own, . . . I was twenty-one. So I threw the
> books in the sea.

This self-conscious, symbolic ritual, related in *The Big Sea,*
re-enacts the drama of the spirited young man rebelling against
his environment, ready to search for his true self. Here are
shades of Melville at sea, Thoreau at Walden, D. H. Lawrence
on his "savage pilgrimage," Joyce on the Continent. Hughes
could not have wanted to see his entire past awash in Lower
Bay: he had had too few Negro playmates and had formed no
lasting friendships, but he had written durable poems. Ironically,
his sense of reality so emphatic in his poems and tentative in his
experience drove him toward the big sea, toward Africa, toward
the proof of strange—and therefore conceivably better—worlds.

Africa was but his first stop in adventures abroad that were
to end in November, 1924. The *Malone* visited thirty-odd ports
along the West Coast, from Dakar in Senegal down to Luanda.
The effect of Hughes's first glimpse of Africa is described in
The Big Sea: ". . . when I saw the dust-green hills in the sunlight,
something took hold of me inside. My Africa, Motherland of
the Negro peoples! And me a Negro! Africa! The real thing.
. . . [The next day, farther south] . . . it was more like the
Africa I had dreamed about—wild and lovely, the people dark
and beautiful, the palm trees tall, the sun bright. . . ." Hughes's
attachment to Africa, largely expressed in later nonfiction,
worked its way into a dozen or so poems, written mostly in the
next few years. The earliest public fruit of his voyage was the

article "Ships, Sea, and Africa," published in *The Crisis* (December, 1923). None of his stories explore African life except "African Morning" (first published as "Outcast" in *The Pacific Weekly* of August 31, 1936), which uses the plight of a mulatto boy, Edward, whom Hughes had met while a sailor on the *Malone*.

The one substantial expression in fiction of that voyage is practically unknown. It is found in "Luani of the Jungles" and in what I have named the West Illana Series—composed of three stories published in 1927 by Harlem's *The Messenger:* "Bodies in the Moonlight" (April), "The Young Glory of Him" (June), and "The Little Virgin" (November).[5] Because they are autobiographical, seven characters are each traceable to the *Malone's* crew of forty-two. All ports but one covered by the fictional *West Illana* were visited by the *Malone,* and the near-starvation and bawdy sexual forays of *West Illana* sailors reflect Hughes's months at sea. Even red Jocko, the biting, phonograph needle-spitting monkey the author brought from Africa, has a role. In these stories, Hughes manages a partial evocation of the Africa he felt. The cocked cap of a sailor presides over this narrow world of sea, ship, and coastal town, despite imbedded themes of innocence, beauty, poetry, and the search for love and manhood. To be shown that a sailor's life is more than salty froth and brawl, one must wait, however, for "Red-Headed Baby" and "Sailor Ashore."

By Christmas, 1923, the *Malone's* whole crew having been fired, Hughes was employed on a freighter running between Holland and New York. Within two months he was standing in the Gare du Nord in Paris, a stranger with only seven dollars. Befriended by a Russian dancer named Sonya, he secured two jobs in night clubs, the second as dishwasher at the famous Grand Duc on the Rue Pigalle. There he heard blues and jazz played by top Negro musicians: Cricket Smith, Buddy Gilmore, and others.

Hughes moved from his room in Montmartre, shared by Sonya before she left in March for Le Havre, to a rooming house near the Place Clichy. It was like a dream, he writes in *The Big Sea,* "living in a Paris garret, writing poems and having champagne for breakfast." Then he fell in love. Mary, a brown-skinned beauty whose family traveled on business between Nigeria and London, wanted to elope to Florence. But while Hughes was calculating his negligible means, a Negro doctor arrived to rush Mary back to London; his mission for her father had apparently been prompted by a letter from Mary's Jamaican roommate.

Later Hughes transformed his last memory of Mary, seated in his attic exchanging with him fresh strawberries dipped in cream, into a charming poem, "The Breath of a Rose." It appeared in *The Big Sea* and was later set to music by William Grant Still. The lyric compares love to dew fading on lilacs, to starlight dying at dawn. It ends:

> Love is like perfume
> In the heart of a rose:
> The flower withers,
> The perfume goes—
>
> Love is no more
> Than the breath of a rose.
> No more
> Than the breath of a rose.

The vicissitudes of night-club life struck the Grand Duc after Florence Embry left to open the Chez Florence. The vagaries of the scullery raised Hughes to the title of waiter, aided by the belligerent insistence of Bruce, the giant one-eyed cook. And poetic advancement came in the form of Dr. Alain Locke, who visited to obtain poems for a special issue of *Survey Graphic*. During the four months that passed before Hughes's return to Harlem, he was invited to Italy by two friends who had taught him how to wait table at the club. Later he accepted Dr. Locke's invitation to see Venice. While recrossing Italy by train, he suffered a reversal of fortunes at the hands of a pickpocket who fathomed the Kansas trick of pinning one's wallet in an inside coat pocket. Hughes became a hungry beachcomber at Genoa —a plight that gave origin to a work of poetic prose complementing the West Illana Series.

Ejected one morning from the local flophouse, the Albergo Populare, Hughes sank upon a park bench, wrote "Burutu Moon," and sent it to *The Crisis* with a request for twenty dollars to ward off starvation. This piece, with flowing, tableau-like scenes describing two sailors' moonlight sojourn through peaceful Burutu on the Nigerian delta, was later modified as a chapter of *The Big Sea*. When the twenty dollars arrived,

Hughes was already an unpaid workaway on a freighter headed for Naples, Palermo, Valencia, and finally New York.

V *The Harlem Renascence*

After arriving in Harlem on November 24, 1924, and buying cigarettes, Hughes had five cents left in his pocket. But his delayed earnings from "Burutu Moon" paid his way to Washington, D. C., where his mother and half-brother Kit were living with the influential branch of the family descended from Congressman John M. Langston. Hughes found a job at a wet-wash laundry, his only alternative to the unobtainable position of page-boy at the Library of Congress, deemed suitable by relatives. His next job, as clerk for the Association for the Study of Negro Life and History, was an upward social tilt; but he quit to work at the Wardman Park Hotel.

That hotel has special meaning. There, in December, 1925, the bus boy saw Vachel Lindsay dining; and Hughes unobtrusively laid copies of three of his own poems beside the poet's plate: "Jazzonia," "Negro Dancers," and "The Weary Blues." The next morning at the hotel, newspapermen were waiting with notebooks and cameras, for Lindsay had informed Washington that he had discovered a Negro bus-boy poet. He had also left a note of advice, including the admonition to "hide and write and study and think." But Hughes could not hide. At the behest of the headwaiter, he often had to submit to the leisurely scrutiny of curious guests at their table. He quit the hotel and took his last job in Washington, a stint behind the counter of a fish and oyster house.

While living in Washington, Hughes took several trips to New York, where, the very night of his return from Europe, at an NAACP benefit party he had met Walter White, Mary White Ovington, James Weldon Johnson, and Carl Van Vechten. During these trips Hughes met practically all the Negro writers who were prominent during what has usually been called "the Harlem Renascence."[6] He knew Jean Toomer, Eric Walrond, Rudolph Fisher. He knew other "New Negro" writers: Countee Cullen, Zora Hurston, Arna Bontemps, Wallace Thurman, and Nella Larsen, to mention a few. He also met the people who encouraged them: Charles S. Johnson, editor of *Opportunity*, who, Hughes remembers, probably "did more to encourage and develop Negro writers during the 1920's than anyone else in America"; and Jessie Fauset. These two and Alain Locke, Hughes writes, "midwifed the so-called New Negro literature into being."

What Hughes's trips meant, what Harlem meant, and what the author's Washington and Lincoln University days owed to the relative nearness of that "black metropolis" cannot be comprehended without some graphic reference to the glitter of the most fantastic decade Harlem has ever known—one that started with *Shuffle Along, Running Wild,* and the Charleston and that ended with the stock market crash of 1929.

The Harlem Renascence shared the exuberance of the Roaring Twenties. When the heiress A'Lelia Walker, "joy-goddess of Harlem's 1920's," died, De Lawd from *Green Pastures*—actually the Reverend A. Clayton Powell—stood over the casket. At Florence Mills's funeral an airplane released flocks of blackbirds overhead. The charlatan revivalist, the Reverend Dr. Becton, had two valets and used a jazz band as background for sermons. Night life was uninhibited. The Cotton Club on Lenox Avenue catered to gangsters and rich whites. Lindyhoppers at the Savoy made up acrobatic routines to please similar trade, and the floor there was built to rock as the dancers swayed. Gladys Bentley played hypnotic piano music all night long in a small club.

Stunning parties were common. Silver-turbaned, dark-skinned A'Lelia Walker entertained at her Harlem apartment or at her mansion at Irvington-on-the-Hudson, attracting Witter Bynner, Muriel Draper, and Lady Nancy Cunard wearing twelve bracelets. Van Vechten's parties, reported in Negro society columns, took place on West 55th Street "in a Peter Whiffle apartment, full of silver fishes and colored glass balls and ceiling-high shelves of gaily bound books," writes Hughes in *The Big Sea;* they offered entertainment ranging from Indian war dances, drums, and blues, to arias straight from the Metropolitan Opera. Guests included Madame Helena Rubinstein, Richmond Barthe, Salvador Dali, and Waldo Frank. Through Van Vechten, Hughes met Somerset Maugham, Hugh Walpole, Fannie Hurst, and Louis Untermeyer.

Parties more literary were given by V. F. Calverton, Horace Liveright, Alfred A. Knopf, and Arthur Spingarn. Some Negroes catered to young guests: Aaron Douglass, for example, and Jessie Fauset. James Weldon Johnson entertained such solid people as the Clarence Darrows, while Wallace Thurman took in bohemians from Greenwich Village and Harlem. Interracial mingling was common: "George" meant George Gershwin, and Theodore Dreiser could sometimes be seen in night clubs in Harlem.

The vogue spread to books, African sculpture, music, dancing. Names now famous became known for the first time: Roland Hayes, Paul Robeson, Bessie Smith, Ethel Waters, Louis Armstrong, Josephine Baker, Duke Ellington, Bojangles, Claude McKay. Each season at least one Broadway hit had a Negro cast, and books by Negro authors sold well.

Hughes as a writer cannot, of course, be explained by references to the Harlem Renascence. But one cannot overlook the imponderable effect of these scintillating years on a young writer who came to know most of the talented Negroes lured to Harlem and the influential white publishers and artists who took an interest in them.

VI   Lush Years: The Weary Blues, Fine Clothes, and Not Without Laughter

The first prize for "The Weary Blues" received by Hughes in 1925—his "America" simultaneously won third prize—was followed by more awards in the lush years that remained before the Wall Street catastrophe. He won an Amy Spingarn prize from *The Crisis,* and "A House in Taos" took first prize in Witter Bynner's Intercollegiate Undergraduate Poetry Contest in 1926. A scholarship enabled Hughes to attend Lincoln University, an unusual Christmas gift from a benevolent New York woman.

In 1925, a year when Hughes wrote many poems,[7] "Minstrel Man" and "Cross" appeared with four other poems in the December issue of *The Crisis.* That year, too, he received his first check, for $24.50, for three poems selected by *Vanity Fair.*[8] In May, 1926, "Youth" appeared on the cover of Chapel Hill's *The Orange Jewel.* That October the cover of *Opportunity* bore his "Feet o' Jesus." *The Crisis* printed "Ma Lord" in June, 1927. Each work turned out to have particular meaning in the whole body of Hughes's poetry. These and other poems had appeared in at least twenty-five different periodicals by the end of 1929, and he had also published four book reviews by then. In this period he wrote his first book introduction, one for *A Little Book of Central Verse.*

Hughes's popularity as a poet now justified publication of a volume. Alfred A. Knopf, Inc., to whose attention his poetry had been brought by Van Vechten (who also recommended his works to Margaret Case of *Vanity Fair*), brought out two collections by Hughes during the Harlem Renascence: *The Weary Blues* (1926) and *Fine Clothes to the Jew* (1927). Van Vechten, to whom the second volume was dedicated, wrote the introduction to the first. Reviews of the first volume, largely favorable, praised the poems for their lifelike directness, vividness, and spontaneity; and they generally approved the unusual exploration of Negro experience and the blues. Most of the reviewers preferred "The Weary Blues," "Negro Dancers," "Sea Calm," "Cross," "Proem" (later entitled "Negro"), "Blues Fantasy," and "Song for a Banjo Dance."

In the few pages of *The Big Sea* that comment on *Fine Clothes,* Hughes largely confines himself to the unfavorable reviews in Negro newspapers. Captions like "Langston Hughes— the Sewer Dweller" and epithets like "the poet low-rate of Harlem" are indeed eye-catching, but literary exposure of low-class Negroes has long been frowned upon by some Negro critics. It is worth pointing out details, however, to which Hughes merely alludes. Most Negro and white reviewers approved the blues poems, the revelations of Negro working-class life (giving rise among reviews to the attributive *proletarian*), and the general craftsmanship. Hughes was considered a modernistic seeker of new verse forms, a potentially major American poet. Some disagreement centered upon his use of dialect and upon the limitations of the blues. The jazz poems, though praised a little more than those in *The Weary Blues,* still eluded the analytical machinery of the reviewers, who as a group preferred *Fine Clothes.*

Hughes, too, preferred his second volume, he says in *The Big Sea,* "because it was more impersonal . . . and because it made use of the Negro folk-song forms, and included poems about work and the problems of finding work. . . ." He commented further when writing to Dewey R. Jones of *The Chicago Defender:* "It's harder and more cynical . . . and it's limited to an interpretation of the so-called 'lower classes,' the ones to whom life is least kind. I try to catch the hurt of their lives, the monotony of their 'jobs,' and the veiled weariness of their songs. They are the people I know best."[9] Reviewers thought the best poems in this volume were "Song for a Dark Girl," "Feet o' Jesus," "Homesick Blues," "Mulatto," "Brass Spittoon," "Porter," and a few others of less merit.

Hughes gave his first poetry reading at John Haynes Holmes Community Church in New York in 1923 after Augustus Granville Dill, business manager of *The Crisis,* who attended the church, had prepared the way. He read next in Washington, D.C., at The Playhouse, on January 15, 1926, under the auspices of The Playwriter's Circle. Alain Locke presided. Later that year, Hughes read in New York, Baltimore, Philadelphia, Cleveland, Indianapolis, and other cities.

The young author's most conventional experience of the 1920's rounded out the decade: his four years at Lincoln University, forty miles from Philadelphia. He satisfied the students' hazing requirements by barking at the moon, crawling on his stomach around the circumference of the campus, and enduring the normal sequence of beatings. In deference to his reputation, the sophomores insisted that he dance the Charleston while they solemnly chanted "The Weary Blues."

The summer after his first year at Lincoln, he joined six other Negro writers in New York to publish "a Negro quarterly of the arts" entitled *Fire,* but most of the single issue was later destroyed by a basement fire. And he labored almost nightly on one of his strongest poems, "Mulatto." The next summer, the year of the great flood used in Faulkner's *Old Man,* found Hughes reading poems at Fisk University and preparing to tour the South—including New Orleans, from where he made an unexpected trip to Cuba as mess boy on a freighter. He joined Zora Neale Hurston on a folklore society hunt for Southern conjure men, former slaves, and folk guitarists. Returning to Lincoln as a sophomore, he began a technique for which he was to become widely known: he read his poems at Princeton to the background music of the Lincoln University Glee Club.

After his junior year, Hughes turned novelist. In the summer of 1928 he decked the dormitory walls with imagined histories of characters to be used, then wrote the novel in six weeks. He reworked it in his senior year and the following summer; and after an autumn trip to Canada he revised it in Westfield, New Jersey. *Not Without Laughter* (1930), with its restrained, simple revelation of the life of a Negro boy in a small Kansas town, received complimentary reviews in the press of New York, London, and Melbourne. But in the United States and elsewhere, praise was tempered with notice of structural defects and undramatic action.

VII *"Things Fall Apart": Travel in the Caribbean and the U.S.S.R.*

Little in Hughes's life just after the stock market crash foretold the collapse of his private world. *The Big Sea* counts his blessings: ". . . I found myself with an assured income from someone who loved and believed in me, an apartment in a suburban village for my work . . . boxes of fine bond paper . . . a filing case, a typist . . . and wonderful new suits of dinner clothes . . . and a chance to go to all the theaters and operas. . . ." This largesse from an elderly Park Avenue white woman to whom he had been introduced in 1928 flowed from an attitude deeply sincere but mistaken in its reasons for benevolence. The slowly revealed incompatibility in the basic beliefs of Hughes and his patroness is told in *The Big Sea:* ". . . she felt that [Negroes] were America's great link with the primitive, and that they had something very precious to give to the Western World. She felt that there was mystery and mysticism and spontaneous harmony in their souls, but that many of them had let the white world pollute [them]. . . ." A later paragraph reveals Hughes's response to her expectations: ". . . I did not feel the rhythms of the primitive surging through me, and so I could not live and write as though I did. I was only an American Negro—who had loved the surface of Africa and the rhythms of Africa—but I was not Africa. I was Chicago and Kansas City and Broadway and Harlem."

Delights, doubts, and finally a sickening frustration marked his transitional year, 1930. While he rode behind a white chauffeur in his patroness's town car, depression-bent, hungry Negroes walked by. When his benefactress was displeased by his bluntly satirical poem, "Advertisement for the Waldorf-Astoria" (which jabbed at poverty by references to the "black mob from Harlem," the "thousand nigger section hands," and the rubber plantation laborers who toiled "for rich behinds to ride on thick tires"), Hughes must have known that for him, too, a lush decade had ended. As he sat in her drawing-room for the last time in December of 1930,[10] becoming sick at the stomach just as he had in Toluca in 1919, he could have felt no solace other than the inevitability of his actions. "I asked kindly," he says in *The Big Sea,* "to be released from any further obligations to her, and that she give me no more money, but simply let me retain her friendship." His patroness, whom he has never identified, according to her wish, withdrew her good will along with her money.

By the fall of 1933, Hughes had found a new opportunity to write without financial worries. The interim was enlivened by enough adventure and travel to lighten his troubles, and he faced those years as a professional writer. His determination shows at the end of *The Big Sea:* ". . . I'd had a scholarship, a few literary awards, a patron. But those things were ended now. . . . I determined to make [my living] writing. I did. Shortly poetry became bread; prose, shelter and raiment. Words turned into songs, plays, scenarios, articles, and stories." To him, "Literature is a big sea full of many fish. . . ." This decision, although it documents Hughes's longevity as a professional, does not provide a date for the measurement of his literary growth. He knew his purposes and subject near the start of his career. In May, 1964, he remarked humorously at an autograph party for contributors to his *New Negro Poets: U.S.A.* that his "trend of thought" as a writer had not changed since he was fifteen.

In 1931, Hughes went to Cuba and Haiti, using most of the four hundred dollars he had received from the 1931 Harmon Gold Award for Literature, given him for *Not Without Laughter.* He then made a nine-month poetry reading tour across America, but he cancelled his final appearances for May, 1932, to join a Harlem group of twenty-two Negroes, mostly writers and students, on a movie-making trip to Russia. In the Caribbean, Hughes associated with various writers and artists, among them Nicolás Guillén in Cuba and Jacques Roumain, who became Haiti's most famous writer. On his American tour, he met folklorist E. C. L. Adams and the Mississippi poet, Will Alexander Percy. He spent an hour at Straight College in New Orleans encouraging the young poet Margaret Walker, who later won the Yale Younger Poets Award with *For My People.* His most fortunate meeting was with Noel Sullivan, whose home atop San Francisco's Russian Hill, formerly the mansion of Robert Louis Stevenson, became his base while he lectured on the Coast.

And Lincoln Steffens, Sullivan's old friend, read Hughes's poems and gave him advice on travel in the Soviet Union.

On that fifteen-month trip abroad, after the August cancellation of Meschrabpom Films' unrealistic movie *Black and White,* the Negro would-be actors dispersed. Hughes traveled widely in the Soviet Union before leaving for home in June, 1933, via Korea, Tokyo, Shanghai, and Honolulu. In the Soviet Union his many experiences familiarized him with exotic places like Samarkand, Ashkhabad, and ancient Bokhara. He nearly froze while visiting cotton collectives in Uzbekistan; he nearly roasted crossing the desert with Arthur Koestler in an old Ford bound for Permetyab; and he was vexed by the love-making rituals of a leather-skinned Tartar girl in Tashkent. Besides Koestler, whose laconic reminder, "a writer must write," spirited Hughes into creative work in Ashkhabad, he encountered other literary people and experiences. He met Boris Pasternak for a quiet, memorable chat. He found Tokyo magazines containing translations of his poems and Orientalized drawings of his face. In Shanghai *Not Without Laughter* was being translated, and in Central Asia *The Weary Blues* was being translated into Uzbek. During Hughes's absence, Knopf in New York had published *The Dream Keeper*, a book of poems especially for young people and selected largely from his first two volumes. Among the new poems, reviewers favored the title piece, written when Hughes was about twenty-two.[11]

His determination to live by writing was strengthened now by successes mentioned in *I Wonder As I Wander*. He earned enough, he writes, from articles on Asia sold to *Izvestia, International Literature,* and other Moscow publications to "travel all over the Soviet Union, to come home via Japan and China, and to live . . . at what were equivalent to [first-class] hotels in America." His fiction was promising too: ". . . I sent my first three stories from Russia to an agent [Maxim Lieber][12] in New York, and by the time I got back to America he had sold all three. . . . And once started, I wrote almost nothing but short stories."

VIII *The 1930's:* The Ways of White Folks and *The Negro Theater*

When the *Taiyo Maru* docked in San Francisco in August, 1933, Hughes was driven to Noel Sullivan's flower-covered house on Hyde Street. Sullivan, Hughes tells in *I Wonder*, kindly listened during a luncheon: "I told my host of my hopes to complete a series of short stories. . . . Sullivan offered me his cottage at Carmel-by-the-Sea . . . for a year, with a houseboy in attendance. This generous offer I accepted gratefully." Under such ideal circumstances, Hughes wrote some of his best stories at the cottage, called "Ennesfree." Partly spurred on by the medical expenses of his mother, now in Oberlin, Ohio, he worked ten or twelve hours daily on both stories and articles. As described by Hughes, each story treated "some nuance of the race problem," and each originated in actual situations he had heard of or been involved in; but he changed the characters beyond recognition by the real participants.

The first nine stories written during the Carmel period and five written in Moscow comprised *The Ways of White Folks* (1934).[13] Surveying ninety-one reviews, one finds their largest consensus in their approval of the easy, natural artistry, as well as the variety and comprehensiveness of subject. The stories, with settings ranging from Alabama to the Middle West, from Florida to New England, and from Harlem to Paris, were said to reveal "the whole plight of the Negro." Some bitterness of tone was noted, but so were the restraint and humor. Opinions varied as to the presence of propaganda, "sociological case work," and extremist characterization,

Between the fall of 1934 and that of 1935, Hughes lived and wrote in places other than Carmel. After a month in a Negro boardinghouse in Reno, he learned from a telegram that his father had died while he himself had been writing, about November 20, 1934, what he later thought of as a psychically inspired story, "Mailbox for the Dead."[14] He borrowed money from his Aunt Sally in Indianapolis to go to Mexico City for the reading of the will that, as he had expected, left him nothing. The sole legatees, the three elderly spinster Patiño sisters, who had been his father's only friends, insisted that he share his father's bank deposits. After repaying his aunt, he was stranded in Mexico.

With his characteristic ability to accept life with joy, Hughes turned the early months of 1935 into a delightful season. He read *Don Quixote* in the original, translated Mexican stories and poems, and watched bullfights every week. By springtime, earnings from stories enabled him to share a small apartment with the French photographer Henri Cartier-Bresson and the Mexican poet Andres Henestrosa. About to be lionized after publicity in *El Nacional,* Hughes left in June for Los Angeles, where he and his friend since the Renascence days, Arna Bontemps, spent several weeks collaborating on their Haitian children's book. Moving to Carmel again, Hughes soon received a troubling letter from his mother, now a victim of cancer. His dutiful trip to Oberlin practically exhausted his funds from the Guggenheim Fellowship he had been awarded that year.

Hoping to advance his career, particularly through sales of his new stories and articles, Hughes went to New York in September. He was surprised to find his play, *Mulatto,* written five years earlier at Jasper Deeter's Hedgerow Theater, scheduled to open October 24. Changed by the producer, Martin Jones, from the "poetic tragedy" Hughes had intended into a melodrama with more emphasis on sex, the play ran for a year on Broadway, then toured the country for two seasons.

Banned in Philadelphia, *Mulatto* dramatized a fatal conflict between a college-educated mulatto youth and his white father in Georgia. It established a record, among plays written by Negroes, for the number of performances in America. Publicized in New York by a picturesque "Southern colonel" striding down Broadway bearing a sign calling the play "a lewd and licentious lie and an insult to the Southern aristocracy," *Mulatto* was widely reviewed. Most critics called it artless, interesting, or sincere. Phrases like "several intensely dramatic scenes," "amazing impartiality," "not yet a capable playwright," "merely another special plea," and "suffers from bad direction" also indicate the diversity of the critics' response. This first play of Hughes's to be professionally produced was not printed in English before the author's version appeared in Webster Smalley's *Five Plays by Langston Hughes* (1963).

Hughes progressed little in 1936 and the first half of 1937. He lived mostly in Cleveland, supporting his ailing mother there and paying his half-brother's tuition at Wilberforce College. But income from his writings was small, and he collected his royalties from *Mulatto* only after extensive intervention by the Dramatists Guild. Fortunately, the Baltimore *Afro-American* offered him four to six months abroad to cover the activities of Negroes fighting in the Spanish Civil War in the International Brigades. Offers by the *Cleveland Call-Post* and the *Globe* magazine to buy articles on the war improved his prospects even more.

Hughes did his job well—in Barcelona, Valencia, and Madrid; in the American Base Hospital; and at the Ebro front. Because he was an American, like Hemingway, he was given a well-exposed, top-floor hotel room in Madrid, facing the Franco batteries; and he was later wounded by a piece of dum-dum bullet. At his naïvest, he listened to cheeps of birds that turned out to be the whiz of bullets. At his hungriest, before eating his ration of snails, he listened to Franco's broadcasts of dinner menus at Seville and Burgos hotels. He saw his first Moor, who inspired a nine-stanza poem in his "Letters from Spain" series. The middle stanza of the poem (in Madrid's *The Volunteer for Liberty*, November 15, 1937) reads:

> And as he lay there dyin'
> In a village we had taken,
> I looked across to Africa
> And I seen foundations shakin'. . . .

Among the letters he received in Spain, several were from Elsie Roxborough in Detroit, "the girl I was in love with then," Hughes writes in *I Wonder*. She had staged his *Drums of Haiti*, whose other titles were, at various times, *Emperor of Haiti* and *Troubled Island*. Her letters dwindled, then disappeared—just as she herself, often mistaken for white, had disappeared from the Negro race before he returned.

Back in New York in January, 1938, Hughes felt the momentum which the success of *Mulatto* had given him before the trip to Spain. At this point in his career (where his biographical trail grows dim in the absence of an autobiographical or other substantial narrative record beyond 1937), Hughes could look back upon several productions of his plays, like those of *Troubled Island, Little Ham,* and *When the Jack Hollers* (written with Bontemps) in 1936; *Drums of Haiti, Joy to My Soul,* and *Soul Gone Home* in 1937. These had been performed by the Gilpin Players of Cleveland's Karamu House, the 1915 settlement house ("a ramshackle house of magic," some called it) later guided by Russell and Rowena Jelliffe to prominence as an art center for young Negroes.

Hughes plunged into the challenge of founding a Negro theater with unpaid community actors. Beginning in a second-story Harlem loft and owning no more properties than could be dropped into a small suitcase, excluding the rickety piano, the project was named the "Harlem Suitcase Theater." On April 21, 1938, it gave its first performance at 317 West 125th Street: Hughes's long, one-act historical play *Don't You Want to Be Free?* and two other dramas.[15] This panoramic play, for which Hughes, as executive director of the theater, used advanced techniques he had admired at Oklopkov's and at the Kamery Theater in Russia, evoked spontaneous participation by the audience and achieved a record run of a hundred and thirty-five weekend performances within two years. It treats the Negroes' enslavement, emancipation, violent persecution, and ultimate union with white workingmen. It interfuses spirituals, work chants, jazz, and some of Hughes's blues poems. Possibly the first instance of arena staging in New York, the performance initiated into acting some Negroes who later became well known, among them Earl Jones, Sr.

These plays, together with *Front Porch,* staged in 1938, form a group of works that develop two of Hughes's characteristic themes. Urban Negro folk life is one theme, seen in *Little Ham, When the Jack Hollers,* and *Joy to My Soul,* with some deviation into higher social levels in *Front Porch,* and with tragicomic variation through fantasy in *Soul Gone Home,* in which the corpse of a Negro prostitute's son addresses his mother before the white ambulance attendants arrive. The other plays, about the rebel slave Dessalines, advance the theme of Negro history by dramatizing fifteen years in the career of the liberating black emperor.

In early 1939, Hughes moved to California, where he founded The New Negro Theater in Los Angeles in March. While his recent Harlem associates were preparing to try out *The Organizer,* a folk opera by Hughes and James P. Johnson, and scheduling his adaptation of Lope de Vega's *Fuente Ovejuna,* Hughes's Los Angeles group opened its first season with *Don't You Want to Be Free?* and with his satirical skits, *Em-Fuehrer Jones* and *Limitations of Life.* Hughes spent the rest of his year or more in California grappling with old and new challenges. He put together his fifth collection of poems, drafted his first autobiography, and, with the Negro actor Clarence Muse, spent the spring and summer of 1939 in Hollywood on the precedent-breaking job of writing the scenario and some of the songs for *Way Down South,* a movie starring Bobby Breen.[16] By the autumn of 1940, although Hughes evidently felt like a Harlemite and had a forwarding address on St. Nicholas Avenue, he was in

Carmel Valley near Monterey, California, writing at Hollow Hills Farm. Noel Sullivan had once more come to his aid, letting him use a cottage at one edge of his farm. With the autobiography out of the way, Hughes worked on stories later collected in his second volume, *Laughing to Keep from Crying.*

The Big Sea was published near the start of his residence at Hollow Hills Farm. Reviewers proclaimed the literary, socio-logical, and even psychological value of the autobiography. They called it friendly, anecdotal, picaresque. They saw it as an impartial, entertaining revelation of the not too chaotic childhood and the adventurous ramblings of a young Negro writer. One or two wished that he had recorded more of his soberest reflections, but most of them acknowledged the author's candid insights into an unusual era.

After his stay at Hollow Hills Farm, enhanced by a Rosenwald Fellowship for creative work, Hughes in late 1941 headed for Chicago,[17] where he founded, for the third time, a Negro theatrical group: the Skyloft Players at the Good Shepherd Community House. The importance of such contributions to the artistic life of America is evidenced by Webster Smalley, Professor of Theater at the University of Illinois, who states in the Introduction to his *Five Plays* that "Negro drama . . . has been, until recently, enriched almost single-handedly" by Hughes.

From the summer of 1942 to early 1947, the author lived at 634 St. Nicholas Avenue in Harlem. He shared a three-room apartment with his "adopted uncle and aunt," Emerson and Toy Harper, friends of his family since Kansas days, the former a musician and composer, the latter a dress designer for theatrical celebrities. Mrs. Harper had designed the costumes for *Don't You Want to Be Free?* in its early Suitcase Theater performances and had also doubled as a member of the cast. In the first part of 1947,[18] the household moved to a three-story brownstone house on East 127th Street in Harlem.

IX *The 1940's: A Poet of War and Peace*

In the early 1940's, Hughes spent much energy on World War II. After the Skyloft Players had produced in the spring of 1942 his full-length musical drama, *The Sun Do Move,* and he had returned to Harlem, Hughes prepared to help fight the war. He wrote jingles, verses and slogans for the Treasury Department's

Defense Savings Staff in June, among them his fifty-eight-line "Defense Bond Blues." In February, 1943, the Writers War Board wrote him that it was depending upon him for a flow of useful items. Often he sent doggerel, but it was effective, like "Don't be a food sissy—/You can live without meat./Don't be so choosy—/We've got Hitler to beat!"[19] He wrote articles on Negro soldiers and the Women's Army Corps, and an essay ("World's Largest Negro Hospital") on Fort Huachuca's Station Hospital No. 1.

Hughes also wrote musical lyrics for the soldiers. W. C. Handy and Clarence Jones wrote the music for his *Go and Get the Enemy Blues;* Elie Siegmeister provided the tune for his *New Wind a-Blowin'*. Sometimes Hughes's landlord picked up his oboe, clarinet, or saxophone to experiment with his nephew's lyrics; in such a way *That Eagle* was produced for a Stage Door Canteen show where Hughes worked as a volunteer waiter. When Toy Harper added her own powers to a joint effort one evening in the spring of 1942, the result was *Freedom Road*, the official troop song for several Negro army units that gained transcontinental publicity.

Hughes rounded out his patriotic creations for 1942-1944 with radio material like "Brothers" (on heroic Negro seamen) and "For This We Fight" (written for a Madison Square Garden freedom rally), and with the poem *Freedom's Plow*. At least one wartime literary service of Hughes developed without his knowledge: in 1944 Dutch Underground forces fighting the Nazis produced anonymously three hundred copies of his poems in the form of a forty-six-page book, *Lament for Dark Peoples and Other Poems*.

During the 1940's, Hughes's works continued to be translated —his novel *Not Without Laughter* became *Pero con Risas* in 1945, for example—and in turn he made, among other efforts, translations with collaborators Mercer Cook and Ben Frederic Carruthers, respectively, of Jacques Roumain's novel *Masters of the Dew* and of poet Nicolás Guillén's *Cuba Libre*. Hughes's own prose found a number of outlets: a dozen articles appeared in *Negro Digest* between 1942 and 1948; ten stories brought checks from one syndicate and two magazines in 1944 alone; and each of the following two years marked the appearance of a book introduction.

This decade saw the metropolitan stage make use of Hughes's

talents. He wrote the lyrics for *Street Scene* (1947), with the book by Elmer Rice and music by Kurt Weill. Working from the text of his own three-act tragedy *Emperor of Haiti*, Hughes created the libretto for the four-act opera *Troubled Island* that New York's City Center Opera Company presented in March, 1949. In this work—America's first top-quality presentation of a full-length opera by Negroes—Hughes was pleased to collaborate with the country's leading Negro composer, William Grant Still.

Hughes's poetry of the 1940's, more voluminous than that of any other decade, appeared mainly in *Shakespeare in Harlem* (1942), *Fields of Wonder* (1947), and *One-Way Ticket* (1949). Other poems reached the public in anthologies for children, on the Asch Recording Company's discs, and in Hughes's thirty-page *Jim Crow's Last Stand*. He and Arna Bontemps included fourteen of his poems in their now standard anthology, *The Poetry of the Negro, 1746-1949*. His *Freedom Train* leveled telling questions at the seven red, white, and blue coaches that in 1947 toured America with historic documents under bulletproof glass.

The press called *Shakespeare in Harlem* melancholy, biting, and grim despite its hilarity and the author's prefatory description of it as "light verse"; reviewers saw it as conscious artistry in control of a refined social sensitivity. Negro historian Carter G. Woodson named the poet a "soldier for human rights," and Louis Untermeyer thought the volume "unquestionably [his] best book." Of *Fields of Wonder*, reviewers generally implied that the many poems reflecting the author's nonracial experience lacked the ardor and the "oceanic turbulence," as one termed it, of his earlier poetry. A few charged his lapse into mellowness and his involvement with the snake, the snail, and the silver rain to the influence of Emily Dickinson, Stephen Crane, or Edwin Arlington Robinson. Others praised the poems about racial exploitation. A few who liked the broader thematic appeal of this volume called Hughes a now more truly American poet.

Of the three volumes, *One-Way Ticket* fared the worst in the press. Some commentators almost wistfully recorded their preference for his earlier works while mildly emphasizing the forbearance, humor, and directness in the poems in the new book. Others labeled the volume "thin and artificial," or they mixed old praise with new blame by observing that his present "jejune and iterative" verse left his reputation still undimmed.

The 1940's added to the series of awards received by Hughes. A thousand-dollar grant came from the American Academy of Arts and Letters in 1946. A different kind of recognition inhered in the position he accepted as poet-in-residence at Atlanta University in 1947 and as a "resource teacher" and counselor at the Laboratory School of the University of Chicago in 1949. More important than campus associations, however, were his almost yearly poetry-reading tours, some covering as many as seventeen states (in 1944), and his commingling with Katherine Anne Porter, Malcolm Cowley, Margaret Walker, Carson McCullers, Morton Zabel, and others at Yaddo in upstate New York. This decade also marked Hughes for archival immortality, at least; for by December, 1949, all of his manuscripts, letters, and other records that he was willing to relinquish were sought by Yale University for its James Weldon Johnson Memorial Collection.

X   *The 1950's: The Dean of Negro Writers*

The 1950's excelled other decades in Hughes's career in the number and variety of books produced. His "Simple" books of this decade established a comic mode more evident in the author's second collection of stories, *Laughing to Keep from Crying* (1952), than it had been in his first. One out of every four reviewers noted the humor and irony in the stories. Twice as many emphasized the breadth of the total picture of Negroes, the absence of propaganda, and the variety. These stories, unlike those of the earlier collection, were generally deemed free from bitterness; but one thoughtful commentator saw "unwavering pessimism" in the volume.

Hughes's opera *The Barrier,* based on one of his earliest stories, "Father and Son," and also evolved from his play *Mulatto,* was presented in January, 1950, by the Columbia University Opera Workshop. Jan Meyerowitz wrote the music for this production, which reached Broadway by November. Shifting next from the writing of librettos to the composition of lyrics, Hughes helped Joe Sherman, Abby Mann, and Bernard Drew create the musical *Just Around the Corner,* performed at the Ogunquit Playhouse in Maine the following year. Later Meyerowitz again wrote the music while Hughes produced the libretto for the opera *Esther,* staged by the University of Illinois in March, 1957, and by Boston's New England Conservatory in 1958. Hughes's musical folk comedy, *Simply Heavenly,* appeared on Broadway in August, 1957. This entertaining show, an early 1955 revision of the book *Simple Takes a Wife,* was made very tuneful by David Martin and was produced in Hollywood in 1957, in London in 1958, and shown on television in the United States for a week in December, 1959. At the time of the premiere of *Simply Heavenly,* the author's Broadway hit of the previous generation, *Mulatto,* was nearing the end of a two-year run in Italy and was about to open in Buenos Aires.

Hughes's work of the 1950's revealed a widening interest in Negro history. He had written historical articles before, such as "A Cuban Sculptor" (*Opportunity,* 1930) and "Maker of the Blues" (*Negro Digest,* 1943). But in this decade he published seven books historical or predominantly historical in treatment, augmented by two collaborative works—*The Sweet Flypaper of Life* (1955) and *A Pictorial History of the Negro in America* (1956)—and by his Folkways phonodisc "The Glory of Negro History." *The New York Times* critic called *The Sweet Flypaper of Life* "probably unique in photographic literature" because of its "perfect union" of Roy De Carava's photographs and Hughes's poetic, folk-style narrative. The almost pocket-sized book contains a story told through an old Negro grandmother whose monologue explores the circumstances of her loved ones and her neighbors. It received excellent reviews, and the pictorial history also earned distinct approval in the press. Its approximately one thousand high-quality illustrations presented the first authoritative panorama of the Negroes' total participation in American life, from the bringing of the first slaves to Virginia in 1619 to the Montgomery bus boycott. The careful research and concise writing of Hughes and Milton Meltzer made this volume a useful reference. It was a timely survey for people unprepared for the Supreme Court decision of May 17, 1954.

Three of the seven historical and biographical books represent most of Hughes's contribution to the First Book Series of Franklin Watts, Incorporated, whose so-called "horizon-pushers" for young people quickly drew praise from child guidance experts, teachers, and librarians. All three received good reviews. His *First Book of Negroes* (1952) anticipated the larger task accomplished by his pictorial history. Using attractive illustrations and the travels of a New York boy to unfold a rather patriotic narrative of famous Negroes and pertinent events, it optimistically answers many questions normal to children in multiracial, color-conscious America. *The First Book of Jazz* (1955), undertaking a harder job, clearly defines technical terms; gives musical-form samples of such specialities as breaks, riffs, and twelve-bar blues; and discusses subjects like "Ten Basic Elements of Jazz." Employing the life of Louis Armstrong as a frame for the evolution of work songs, spirituals, field hollers, minstrel songs, blues, and ragtime (but treating elsewhere other famous jazz musicians), the book encourages a constructive attitude toward jazz. Folkways cut a long-play record, narrated by Hughes, of twenty-seven musical selections to accompany the reading of the book.

The First Book of the West Indies (1956), which has a few minor geographical errors, charmingly compares and contrasts the Antilles: their similar birds and trees, and their differing remnants of Spanish, English, and African customs. Hughes records Caribbean rhythms, gives much economic, cultural, and historical information, and ends his book with a list of eminent people of West Indian birth, including Alexandre Dumas, Toussaint L'Ouverture, and Alexander Hamilton.

The other four books of this decade are more strictly historical except for a collaborative volume on folklore. *Famous American Negroes* (1954) sketches seventeen lives from a dozen or more vocational and professional areas. Hughes acquaints his young readers with persons new to most of them: Dr. Daniel Hale Williams, first surgeon to perform a successful open-heart operation; Ira Aldridge, one of the greatest Shakespearean actors of the nineteenth century; and insurance magnate Charles C. Spaulding, builder of the largest all-Negro business firm in the world.

Famous Negro Music Makers (1955), ranging from banjoes, bones, and popular music to operas and symphonies, destroys some misconceptions about "Negro music." Young readers learn that James A. Bland, the world's greatest minstrel singer, wrote *Carry Me Back to Old Virginny* and *In the Evening by the Moonlight;* that Dean Dixon organized an interracial chamber orchestra and conducted the New York Philharmonic; and that Mahalia Jackson and Bessie Smith both were titled "queens" over rather different realms. The former, singing religious songs, is queen of gospel singers; the latter, with similar voice and delivery, was the "Miss Blues" who in the 1920's and 1930's kept her worshipful audiences weeping and shouting over her Southern blues songs.

Hughes's *Famous Negro Heroes of America* (1958), a 202-page continuation of an extensive subject, tells the memorable and often dangerous roads to fame taken by sixteen Negroes. Readers already initiated can hurry through the pages on Crispus Attucks, who was the first American to die for the nation's liberty, Frederick Douglass, and Harriet Tubman. But they can learn about Gabriel Prosser, the martyred Virginia slave insurrectionist; Robert Smalls, the bold young slave who stole a Confederate ship past Fort Sumter guns into the control of the blockading Union fleet; and Matthew Henson, who planted the American flag at the North Pole forty-five minutes before Admiral Peary arrived.

Collaboration with Arna Bontemps produced *The Book of Negro Folklore* (1958). By ranging from Brer Rabbit to Jesse B. Semple and modern prose in the folk manner, the collection indicates growing Negro acceptance of a still useful ancestral heritage. Its four hundred and thirty-five pages of traditional folklore—stories, rhymes and songs about animals, magic, ghosts, preachers and slavery—combine with little-known but current jokes, jive, and assorted big-city folkways to demonstrate that Negro folk art is unique in some fundamental ways. Through wise and varied selections, Hughes and Bontemps produced the first comprehensive volume of Negro folklore.

Hughes's most interesting nonfiction of the 1950's, from the standpoint of literary history, was his second autobiography: *I Wonder As I Wander,* which covers the years 1931-1937. He writes of his travels with reportorial objectivity and with a sense of warm, human involvement, whether recalling the soup and dirt of a Russian desert or the monthly ceremonial tea at the Pan Pacific Club in Tokyo. The most absorbing parts of the story, told with humor, sympathy, and a democratic love for people, reveal the sense of responsibility Hughes felt as the writer-representative of an oppressed people. They show him both as wandering note taker and as ready participant in a troubled decade on the brink of World War II. He fascinatingly sketches old Emma Harris, the Dixie-born Negro firebrand and black-market hostess of Moscow. He tells with reverent humor how his career as a poet was boosted the hot September days he and Zell Ingram and Mary McLeod Bethune rode eleven hundred miles pressed into the single seat of a small Ford. Through all the personal and social history in the pages glows the essence of the man who was to embody the world's image of a Negro writer.

The relatively small number of new poems by Hughes published in book form during the 1950's compares to his production in the 1930's. His popular *The Negro Mother*, an illustrated paperback of 1958, and his thirteen poems in *Lincoln University Poets* (1954) were not new creations, but *Selected Poems* (1959) contained in its pages some previously unpublished works. *Montage of a Dream Deferred* (1951), Hughes said in its introductory paragraphs, combined into a single "poem on contemporary Harlem" about sixty pages of poetry reprinted from nine periodicals. The poet catches the talk, song, and action of Harlem by forsaking blues patterns and smooth jazz rhythm for the shifting, broken cadences of boogiewoogie and be-bop. A quarter of a century had passed since *The Weary Blues*. Harlem had grown more complex, but Hughes was keeping abreast of the people he had marked for his own.

The lecture platform and other mediums spread Hughes's reputation as a poet in the 1950's. The number of his poetry readings mounted yearly, the pattern of his itinerary varying. He made sixteen appearances in ten weeks, for example, in early 1951, followed by twelve more in the fall; on the other hand, eleven readings in 1953 were spread throughout the year. Piano accompaniment and jazz orchestration continued to support his poetry. Red Allen, the Horace Parlan Quintet, and other musicians backed up Hughes in his reading of "The Weary Blues" and several more poems for an M-G-M phonodisc in 1958. On August 30, 1959, an adaptation of *Shakespeare in Harlem*, with music by Margaret Bonds, played at the White Barn Theater in Westport, Connecticut. (Hughes's review of Avery E. Kolb's novel *Jigger Whitchet's War* appeared the same date in the *New York Herald Tribune*.)

Hughes's sensitivities as a poet enhanced his continued translations, started professionally in Mexico City in early 1935. In 1951, for the *Beloit Poetry Journal*, he went over his translation of *Romancero Gitano* (the "Gypsy Ballads") of Federico García Lorca. In Spain in December, 1937, he had begun translating the fifteen ballads, along with the play, *Blood Wedding*, of the famous Spaniard who had signalized in print his love of Negro music before his murder by the Fascist Falange in 1936. Some reviewers thought his translation not free enough; others, such as the linguist Professor V. B. Spratlin of Howard University, praised Hughes's reproduction of Lorca's music and native imagery.[20]

Indiana University's financially successful publication of his *Selected Poems of Gabriela Mistral* in 1957 brought for the first time to the English-reading public the representative works of this significant Latin-American poet and humanitarian. His exclusion of the three Nobel Prize-winning *Soñetos de la Muerte* ("Sonnets of Death") because of the near-impossibility of faithful translation was perhaps arguable. Certainly relevant was the question of whether any male sensibility could do justice to the intense femininity of most of these rather somber seventy-four poems. Out of fifteen reviewers whose opinions were read for this study, only one took serious exception to the effectiveness of the translation.

Not only did Hughes do some of his best translation in the 1950's, but he also explained, edited, and otherwise commented on poetry. He edited the "Negro Poets Issue" of *Voices* in 1950, and he wrote an introduction for *Japanese Anthology of Negro Poetry* (Tokyo, 1952). In a brief turn to pedagogy, he set down "Ten Ways to Use Poetry in Teaching" for the *CLA Bulletin* in 1951. He added to his juveniles one that must have given him pleasure to write: *The First Book of Rhythms* (1954). This deceptively profound little book no doubt had its origins in his talks to youngsters in the Laboratory School at the University of Chicago, and in similar sessions in the children's rooms of various libraries. Illustrated by Robin King, the book explains the growth of human rhythm from man's primitive realization of his heartbeat, through his drumming, chanting, clapping, and stamping in work and play, to his adaptations of rhythmic principles in the instruments, buildings, and machines of an electronic age.

One of Hughes's last books of the decade was *The Langston Hughes Reader* (1958). A comprehensive, selective anthology, it represents his production in several genres during his publishing career of thirty-odd years. It reveals a meaningful variety in Hughes's attitudes, but knowledge of their evolution through the years, as well as the degree to which they reflect modifications in the viewpoints of Negroes as a whole, does not easily follow the reading of the selections. Lacking an introduction and scholarly addenda, the text was obviously devised to suit popular tastes. A similar comment might be added about his *Selected Poems* of the following year. The collection contains almost all his best poems, but it has no preface, commentary, or apparatus to date the poems or order them chronologically. Like the *Reader*, the collection of poems chosen by the author was not meant to satisfy the demands of literary scholarship.

Hughes's home base remained on 127th Street in Harlem during this productive decade. Sometimes he read and lectured at a university as far away as California; sometimes at a library as distant as Port-of-Spain in the West Indies. But he came back every time to a creative task waiting at his typewriter near an apartment window, third-floor rear, overlooking a Harlem back yard. Usually the task was work on a story. After his spring tour in the South and Midwest in 1950, it was "The Star Decides." After a similar tour in the spring of 1954, it was a double challenge, "A Dialogue at Dawn" and "Thank You, M'am," for each of which he made a third draft on the same historic day: May 17. His writing habits are glimpsed in the fact that he revised five different stories in March, 1957, and in the picture of his making story revisions on the road between Tallahassee and New Orleans in mid-February, 1952. On that trip, made for the twelfth annual Negro History Week, he worked over his still unpublished "Mailbox for the Dead" for the third time—the story first written in 1934 in Reno the night his father had died.[21]

On the threshold of the 1960's, Hughes could feel confidently that his world-wide fame as a poet of the people, as innovator, and as literary spokesman of Negro Americans would endure. Several hundred thousand people had heard him read his poems. College glee clubs had harmonized his verses in neat auditoriums, and jazz bands had rocked and drummed his lines into the all-knowing ears of Negroes who took his meaning without impediment. Poor Negro migrants and urban slum dwellers had guffawed at his stories and Simple newspaper columns, and Negro and white educators had written him letters praising almost all his substantial fiction and nonfiction. His own successful plays, librettoes, and lyrics; the many translations, the musical adaptations, the popular recording of his works; the voluminous correspondence that had proliferated and involved several hundred authors, artists, producers, civic leaders, and celebrities in many fields—all this massive evidence proclaimed his eminence.

CHAPTER 2

The Cult of the Negro

White people
began to come to Harlem
in droves.
—*The Big Sea*

THE PICTURESQUE MOVEMENTS of dark preachers in shouting churches and the frenzy of agile lindyhoppers at the Savoy, mentioned in Chapter 1 as part of the Harlem vogue, had causes and consequences of special literary interest. Behind the entertainment devised for white people lay events that gave the image of the so-called New Negro massive and colorful intensity in Harlem: the wartime migration northward of nearly half a million Negroes, the glorification of blackness by Marcus Garvey, the Freudian enthronement of sex and primitivism, and the exciting study of African art impelled by Picasso, Matisse, Paul Guillaume, Gertrude Stein, and others.

Because of this compelling interest in black people, Harlem lured both the famous and the unknown, the serious and the curious. Some arrived by day, Negroes like Arna Bontemps from California, Countee Cullen from Kentucky, Wallace Thurman from Salt Lake City, and Langston Hughes himself from Washington and points at sea—all believing that the success of the musicals *Running Wild* and *Chocolate Dandies* in 1923, as well as the limelight on Roland Hayes and Paul Robeson, was also destined for them. Some arrived by night, whites mostly from downtown Manhattan, motivated by reading Van Vechten's *Nigger Heaven* or primitivistic works by O'Neill, Waldo Frank, Sherwood Anderson, and DuBose Heyward. Some wanted to glow over a dancing row of brown and golden legs, or to let dusky, laughing Harlemites waft them away from memories of war and remind them that sex was a topic now fashionable to discuss. For these tourists, Harlem was a fad; their image of Negroes was part of a cult, a Northern improvement of the ante-

bellum "happy slave," now modernized by Freudian sophistica-
tion and abundantly available in the flesh a taxi ride away.

I *Poems Behind the Veil*

Hughes's love for Harlem, buoyant even before his first sidewalk acquaintance with it in 1921, and reinvigorated in Paris,
continually brought him to observation posts among the faddish
throngs. Within the year that followed his return from Europe,
he learned that Harlem's glamor was a creature of the night,
a string of lights turned on from lower Manhattan. Only the
music, the dancing, the laughter belonged to Harlem, as completely as possessions that cannot be given away because they
cannot be received. The famous nightclubs, the theaters, and
most of the stores were owned by white people who lived outside of Harlem. Those New Yorkers and tourists who were
driven into the black community after dark knew or cared
nothing of the daytime slum streets and tenements where
Harlemites drudged for a living and could barely afford a
funeral.

Hughes, after a long look at the white mechanism that allowed
Harlem to move about, wrote "Minstrel Man" (in *The Crisis*,
December, 1925):

> Because my mouth
> Is wide with laughter
> And my throat
> Is deep with song,
> You do not think
> I suffer after
> I have held my pain
> So long?
>
> Because my mouth
> Is wide with laughter
> You do not hear
> My inner cry?
> Because my feet
> Are gay with dancing
> You do not know
> I die?

These lines are Hughes's best poetical comment on the cult of
the Negro. Almost as economical and simple as William Blake's
"The Fly," and using only monosyllables except for six words,

this poem conveys the image of a clown held fast in the colorful trap that so entertains an audience bent on seeing only gay contortions. When the face-sized grin is stretched before the reader a second time, after the words *suffer* and *pain,* he knows the elastic, illusory quality of the countenance humanized by the two words. The lines "You do not hear/My inner cry?" urge the reader-spectator to strain his ears for the one sure but barely detectable sign that links mankind. When the reader responds to the image of happily dancing feet, he is vulnerable to the concluding charge ("You do not know/I die?") that his humaneness has become deeply impaired.

Hughes skillfully uses a truth embodied with profound effect a quarter of a century later in the doleful histrionics of Emmett Kelly, the clown. Hughes's remonstrance is softened by its interrogative form, is bare of accusing adjectives, and is given personal immediacy by his fusion of himself with his subject. The added poignancy deriving from implicit historical and contemporary social facts quickens in the reading as long as the minstrel-man tintype of Negro humanity collects dust on American mantelpieces.

Only a few other poems, none written so ably as "Minstrel Man," show how Hughes made literary use of the ironies in this shallow attitude toward Negroes. *Dear Lovely Death* (1931) contains his next-written poem on the subject, "Aesthete in Harlem":

> Strange,
> That in this nigger place,
> I should meet Life face to face
> When for years, I had been seeking
> Life in places gentler speaking
> Until I came to this near street
> And found Life—stepping on my feet!

Written apparently about a Northern city like Manhattan, where the ghetto mentality could coexist with passive tolerance of the accident mentioned in the final verse, the lines suggest the wasteful ignorance fostered by caste and racism. Although the couplets avoid awkwardness and the poem begins and ends in strength, the bulk rests too heavily upon abstractions.

"Death in Harlem," a narrative poem over seven pages long in *Shakespeare in Harlem* (1942), strikes a glancing blow at white addiction to the Negro quarter of Manhattan. It develops the carousing of the Texas Kid and Arabella Johnson in Dixie's place, a swinging bit of low life that ends when Arabella shoots to death a flirtatious girl who misused her absence in the powder room. The faddist attitude toward Negroes is scored in the following lines about the Fifth Avenue whites who enter:

> Dixie grinned. Dixie bowed.
> Dixie rubbed his hands and laughed out loud—
> While a tall white woman
> In an ermine cape
> Looked at the blacks and
> Thought of rape,
> Looked at the blacks and
> Thought of a rope,
> Looked at the blacks and
> Thought of flame,
> And thought of something
> Without a name.

The poet introduces Uncle Tom, but with his charming grin there is the nonracial rubbing of money-making hands. The subsequent use of the color black in an almost diagrammatic pattern with rape, rope, and flame has utter clarity. Yet the reader of poetry, perhaps unreasonably at times, looks for elevation—even when the facts appear to deserve none. The point is Hughes's realistic introduction of downtown whites, like those in many an actual Harlem-bound taxi or limousine. The shooting, a crime of jealousy that closes seriocomic episodes, and itself a subject of the cult that broadcasts Negroes as hazards to themselves over dimes, dice, and frivolous women, is turned against whites by the paired lines quoted. The reader compares the societal meaning of a cheap and fatal, but individual, brawl with that of a pathological, community-inspired lynching.

"Madam and Her Madam" (*Common Ground*, Winter, 1934), a poem on urban Negroes, exhibits a facet of the cult that has long affected economic and social standards. It tells the burdensome variety of hard jobs assigned the protagonist by her white mistress, then ends with the following exchange:

> I said, Madam,
> Can it be
> You trying to make a
> Pack-horse out of me?

She opened her mouth.
She cried, Oh, no!
You know, Alberta,
I love you so!

I said, Madam,
That may be true—
But I'll be dogged
If I love you!

Exaggeration and burlesque dramatize realistic attitudes. The terms "pack-horse" and "I'll be dogged" suitably reflect the circumstances and vocabulary of the maid. The middle stanza, with its false high note and pose of amazed hurt, points at all white people who declare their love for the Negroes they exploit. The opening, "I worked for a woman,/She wasn't mean," shows how gentle whites, when unknowing hosts of the packhorse view of Negro capabilities, can vitiate their own ordinarily considerate natures. The closing lines voice the lesson that surprised thousands of white "madams" in Birmingham, Alabama, when their maids supported the bus boycott of the late 1950's: that Negrophiles delude themselves by expecting affection deeper than that bestowed.

A still later poem concerns generalizations about Negroes. "Theme for English B" (*Common Ground*, Spring, 1949) is about a Columbia University assignment given with the admonition, "And let that page come out of you—/Then, it will be true." The only Negro in the class muses, after considering his identity:

I guess being colored doesn't make me *not* like
the same things other folks like who are other races.
So will my page be colored that I write?
Being me, it will not be white.
But it will be
a part of you, instructor.

.   .   .   .

Sometimes perhaps you don't want to be a part of me.
Nor do I often want to be a part of you.
But we are, that's true!

These prosaic lines say something important about the cult of the Negro. Since terms like "white life" and "Negro life" still resound largely unchallenged in books and articles, perhaps a colored page from a colored student is as logical an academic equivalent; and the protagonist's confidence that, at least, a white page will not issue from a colored student is equally sound. The subsequent two lines of literary miscegenation, though a gratuity to schoolteachers, attack separatism.

The similarity between the last-quoted lines of this poem and the ending of "Madam and Her Madam" reveals Hughes's tendency to turn both sides of the racial coin. In both poems the Negro camp denies that the feelings of white people have any more significance than those of Negroes. The student writing to his white teacher "Nor do I often want to be a part of you" becomes the Negro people reserving for themselves the prerogative to accept or refuse judgments by whites, along with the right to export their own judgments.

II *Short Stories*

Hughes's unanalyzed powers as a short story writer, as compared with his known competence as a poet, may be indicated through examination of the ways in which three of his best stories demonstrate the cult of the Negro. The circumstances of their composition reaffirm the early inevitability of the direction his career was to take. At the start of 1933, separated from the stimulating Harlem Renascence by three depression years and removed from all but a few Negro acquaintances by thousands of miles of ocean and Asian soil, Hughes seemed unlikely to concern himself with Harlem. Yet, Harlem and Negroes were never far from his mind, even in wintry Russia.

That winter, during a rehearsal at the Meyerhold Theater in Moscow, Hughes met a smiling, buxom young actress who, he concluded, had a one-track mind. "Without advance warning," he declared in *I Wonder*, "Natasha simply came to my room in the New Moscow Hotel one night when I was out—and was in bed when I got back." Curiously, this circumstance was a literary problem. The girl was diverting the creative impulses lately roused by D. H. Lawrence's stories, "The Lovely Lady" and "The Rocking Horse Winner," lent him by Marie Seaton of London. Of Natasha's repeated visits, he writes that "I still didn't want an almost nightly guest, the reason being that I had begun writing again, and I always do my best writing at night—alone."

This resumption, near Hughes's thirty-first birthday, actually began his career as a short-story writer. The stories born of this new zeal are entirely different from "Mary Winosky" and the West Illana Series. His new viewpoint is suggested by thoughts that came to him after he wondered how Natasha had gained entrance into his room:

> . . . there are ways of getting almost anywhere you want to go, if you *really* want to go. You might have to squeeze through a knot hole, humble yourself, or drink muddy tea from consumptive bowls or eat camel sausage, pass for a Mexican [all of which Hughes had done], or take that last chance. . . . If you want to see the world, . . . write honest books, or get in to see your sweetheart, you do such things by taking a chance. Of course, a boom may fall and break your neck at any moment, your books may be barred from libraries. . . . It's a chance you take.

Hughes must have known the risk in turning his life more firmly into an unconventional path, in drinking the muddy tea of certain memories and shaping from those depths honest stories about Negroes. He must have remembered lying under the sun in Haiti, mulling over the literary situation in America, and thinking: "The magazines used very few stories with Negro themes, since Negro themes were considered exotic, in a class with Chinese or East Indian features." But such stories, he states in the opening pages of *I Wonder*, were what he wanted to write, even with his patroness estranged, awards scarce, and jobs hard to find: "I did not want to write for the pulps, or turn out fake 'true' stories to sell under anonymous names as Wallace Thurman did. I did not want to bat out slick non-Negro short stories. . . . I wanted to write seriously and as well as I knew how about the Negro people, and make that kind of writing earn for me a living."

1. "Slave on the Block"

Honest stories about Negroes must sooner or later involve white people and racism, and Hughes's stories plunged at once into this engagement. The very first story, "Slave on the Block," written in Moscow in February, 1933,[1] and published that September in *Scribner's Magazine*, is based directly on the Harlem vogue of the 1920's. Speaking of the source of this story in September, 1960, Hughes said, "I knew a couple in Greenwich Village who gushed over Negroes too much—'beyond the call of duty,' " he added with a chuckle. "I wasn't conscious of whom I was writing about." After the story had appeared in *The Ways of White Folks,* the author was horrified to realize that he had used the couple—and was relieved when they said nothing about it. "The characterization is not like them," he explained, "but the facts of their occupation, etc., are true."

In this tale, told in the third person, Michael and Anne Carraway, Village painter and composer for the piano, respectively, rave over and copy "the Art of Negroes—the dancing that had such jungle life about it, the songs that were so simple and fervent, the poetry that was so direct, so real." Their art and record collections, and list of plays to be seen and books to be read, are selected to give them more "darky spirit." They know Harlem through its speakeasies and night clubs; they try hard to make Negro friends, but somehow fail.

The Carraways' fervor is roused anew when in their dark hall they espy Luther, the young nephew of their lately deceased "wonderful colored cook and maid," Emma, whose belongings he is taking away. They almost miss seeing this "marvellous ebony boy" so like the darkness. They hire him, ostensibly to care for their tiny garden, but actually to inspire their art. Anne's first painting, "The Sleeping Negro," refers to the posture necessarily assumed each morning by Luther, exhausted by his steady initiation into Harlem night life by forty-year-old Mattie, the new maid. Anne's second painting, "The Boy on the Block," requires half nude Luther to sit on a box—a pose that so captivates Michael that he joins to her brush strokes his own rather ineffective runs on the piano.

Although paid well and treated nicely, Luther and Mattie do not like the Carraways. To Mattie they are "strange," and Luther, recently from the South, elaborates, "They is mighty funny." Both employees, disliking after-hours work, become unruly. They apparently commiserate with each other in bed, as the Carraways discover when they wake up Luther one night to sing "his own marvellous version of John Henry" for a guest. Anne condones their behavior as "simple and natural for Negroes" and continues to take Lindy Hop lessons from her model.

But Luther increasingly consumes the Carraways' wine and cigarettes, tells jokes on them before their friends; and he and Mattie quarrel more often in the basement, where they openly live together, under a sanction their employers call "liberal-minded." But the Carraways cannot now paint and play with ease. Luther sometimes drags his feet to the model's box, humming an unexpected song that begins "Before I'd be a slave I'd be buried in ma grave."

The climax is induced by Michael's mother, mannish, tall, and bossy. She gets more respect from Mattie than Anne does, but Luther becomes more fractious. He approaches her, shirtless and bearing a red rose, to ask, "How long are you gonna stay in this house?" The mother's scream begins a scene that ends with Luther's dismissal, despite Michael's confusion when his distressed wife reminds him of her unfinished painting—"The Slave on the Block," she calls it this time. As Anne admiringly watches her model go, followed by a vociferous Mattie, she audibly gasps at his ebony body, his "black arms . . . full of roses," and his "beautiful, white-toothed grin."

Hughes, after depicting the shallow interest in Negro art and character shared by this couple, who are among the many who also "went in for Negroes," employs several means to reveal their attitude. They gush through superlatives: Emma was "wonderful"; Luther, "adorable" and "so utterly Negro," knows a "marvellous" folk ballad and sleeps in "delightful simplicity" with Mattie. Metaphors do the same chore: Anne says of Luther, "He *is* the jungle"; her husband avers, "He's 'I Couldn't Hear Nobody Pray.'" Insincere words and actions deepen the portrait: the Carraways, deprived of "poor dear Emma" by death, acquire the "poor, dear boy" Luther.

The falsity of the Carraways' interest is also shown by the servants' reaction to it. Luther and Mattie do not welcome their employers' after-hours attention, generous as it is. The servants, indifferent to the artists, wall themselves in with the belief that "the vagaries of white folks" surpass understanding. And in Harlem at large, whose brightest, gayest corners lure the Carraways by night, the solicitous couple find no friends.

This story shows an important result of modishly superficial involvement with Negroes. The connection between the Carraways' insincerity and their negligence in normal discipline is like the double standard once applied to literature written by Negroes. The Carraways, tolerant of Luther's sleeping and misbehaving on the job, and of their servants' sexual immorality, are lax because the employees do not merit, as human beings, the sincerity that ordinary discipline implies. Significantly, Anne dislikes Mrs.

Carraway, who is the symbol of this discipline that sharpens the theme, and who activates in both servants the feelings that bring the story to a climax. Proof of Luther's and Mattie's humanity—the quarrels and moodiness natural to their "marriage" at work—initially annoys the Carraways and turns their servants into "two dark and glowering people."

"Slave on the Block" has a lightness of touch suitable to the emptiness in the Carraways, which, through them, veils the individuality of Luther and Mattie. The reader does not see either couple in depth, but he does see the flash and bubble that gave frail support to the Harlem craze. The tough realities of Luther's background in the South are only dimly though firmly suggested. One tends to remember a shirtless, dark young man holding a red rose, grinning away—with a curiously hard resolve —the easiest job he will ever have.

2. *"Poor Little Black Fellow"*

"Slave on the Block," the only one of these three tales that treats its theme explicitly, was followed by "Poor Little Black Fellow," written in Moscow in March, 1933. Two months later it was in the hands of *The American Mercury*, which published it in November. In September, 1960, Hughes spoke of its source this way: "I heard of a white couple who had an experience very similar to that in the story. They had trouble when the child got into teenage years."

This third-person narrative explores the cult on a more personal level than the first story. Amanda Lee, like the Carraways' Emma, has been a "perfect servant"; but after her death from pneumonia she leaves, not a grown black nephew, but a six-year-old black son, Arnie. Taking in the child is a Christian duty to a stiff old New England family—not artistic delight to bohemian Villagers—especially since Arnie's father, the Pembertons' stable man, had died fighting for democracy in the Argonne.

The town of Mapleton is proud of the Pembertons' having accepted as their own "poor little black Arnie." He grows up lonely, all Negroes having left the town, despite the citizens' rule that their children be "very nice" to him. And the people are "beset with a Negro problem" when, in their town unexorcised of kissing games and dances, Arnie reaches sixteen. The authorities at the Boy Scout Camp write a personal letter to the Pembertons explaining why they "simply could not admit Negroes." When the Pembertons send him to a Negro charity camp near Boston so that he might know "some of his own people," what Arnie learns he hates: that "black kids from the slums" swear and fight and make fun of outsiders, even black ones.

The Pembertons, nicer than ever, give him two rooms over the garage to entertain the colored friends he does not have. Grace Pemberton prays, her husband consults the Boston Urban League, and her sister Emily questions the church mission board about what to do with Arnie during his last year of high school. Arnie relieves them by promising to get his advanced education at Fisk, a Negro college.

Arnie graduates from high school with high honors; he whiles away the prom joking with boys at the punch bowl; and he stands without a partner to sing the alma mater. To his classmates he is "a lucky chap to be going to Europe"—where the Pembertons plan to give him a nice memory of his life with them. When the steamship company cancels his cabin reservation, the Pembertons take him second class, bearing up "like Christians." When Arnie meets in Paris the famous Negro singer and dancer Claudina Lawrence, he mingles happily with sophisticated Negroes and unbiased Europeans; but the Pembertons are grievously taxed by European ignorance of American propriety. After Arnie stays out all night and turns morose on sightseeing tours, Grace thinks of a remedy—"being very nice to him."

The Pembertons conclude that the devil has gotten into their boy; but the author explains that it is Vivi, the Rumanian girl who plays Chopin. Arnie tracks down her apartment alone. He decides—this time with the devil's aid, the author concedes—to show the Pembertons a white girl who does not care about color. He invites Vivi to dinner at the hotel, where she extends a hand that the stunned New Englanders refuse to see. A rapid Pemberton count of the chairs blindly stops one short of the number required to seat the couple; and the Mapleton consensus, reached soon after Vivi's departure, is that she is a prostitute.

Summoned by Grace, Arnie deliberately hurts her feelings and frowns at a return to prejudiced America. To the family, he declares, after Mr. Pemberton withdraws their protection, "I've always wanted to go." Mapleton conservatism staggers under its final blow: the discovery that "poor little black Arnie" plans to marry Vivi. The husband retorts sarcastically, the sister laughs drily, and the wife faints; but they, like the reader, are unaware of whether the girl has accepted Arnie.

"Poor Little Black Fellow," more consistently serious and more broadly meaningful than "Slave on the Block," pursues the same basic theme. Here the cult is cant, mainly religious, which in the name of Christian duty sanctifies arbitrary limitations on ordinary individual liberty. For years the Pembertons call Arnie "it," maintaining for themselves that remarkable flexibility of attitude usually reserved for pets, so that the bestowal and withdrawal of human considerations is left to whim.

The reader might balk at the suggestion that the Pembertons are insincere. Hughes would approve of such reluctance, for he points out that Grace was "really fond of" Arnie; and he never suggests hostility on the part of Emily or Mr. Pemberton before the final scenes. The Pembertons, then, like nearly all liberals, not to mention others, seemingly are prevented by some complex yet thin-fibered inner obstruction from knowing how to be genuine toward colored people.

This entire strand in the story, effectively tacit and complete in minor phrases and in unemphasized actions, weaves inevitable personal consequences. The Pembertons enmesh themselves in a persistent deceit all the more bewildering because it throws a troublesome cloud over standard virtues. Niceness has no lustre and solves no problems. It keeps Arnie away from the give-and-take of a normal childhood, gives him a pennant-hung but unsocial apartment, buys him half a dozen pretty French ties—and lodges in his benefactors' files a pleasant letter of refusal. But, in doing each, niceness either postpones necessity or avoids human service.

A more corrosive self-deceit threads the Christian duty of the Pembertons. Just as Mapleton cannot distinguish between pride in Arnie and pride in its own charity, the Pembertons cannot distinguish between a family responsibility and a problem for the Boston Urban League. Although metamorphosed from an "it," Arnie is not yet a person, a fact demonstrated in the family response to Arnie's awakening in Paris: never do the adults who have reared the youngster recognize in his sullen behavior the signs of advanced adolescence. His color adequately explains all, just as it links his contemplated advanced education automatically with Fisk, "where those dear Jubilee singers sang so beautifully."

Hughes condenses the meaning of his story after Arnie is made happy by his meeting with Claudina: "Somebody had offered him something without charity, without condescension, without prayer, without distance, and without being nice." The stifling nature of Arnie's life with the Pembertons is subtly revealed by the fact that Hughes does not allow him to speak until this meeting with the tan beauty, halfway through the story. Although this technique has a logic of its own, the author, according to his comments on the point, did not consciously use it.[2]

Hughes handles important consequences of bigotry indirectly (roughly eighty-five per cent of such references are allusive): the Pembertons are undisturbed by Claudina's fame until she moves next door to them; they resent the well-dressed appearance of Parisian Negroes; and they feel that the home town that has been "proud" of Arnie and has granted him high honors at graduation cannot allow him a satisfactory adult life. Bigotry leads to deterioration in character when the Pembertons are rude to Arnie's friend, Vivi; it leads to a perversion of judgment when they conclude that only a whore could become interested in the boy they have reared. For Arnie, it leads finally to a pernicious but familiar dichotomy when he tells Vivi that the Pembertons are not his parents, but are white people.

Hughes's few explicit references to bigotry are less successful artistically. When Arnie tells Vivi "how hard it was to be black in America," the reader detects a flaw: the truth of the boy's words is not a product of his own life. He knows how hard it has been for him to be black in Mapleton, but the schools and people of that village could have given him scant knowledge of the complex, historical meaning of being black in America at large. Yet, the talk of the two youngsters gives bigotry world-wide meaning; and, through Vivi's innocently ambiguous words of solace, "All old people are the same," Hughes offers the torch to the young.

Certain elements of style found in this story are typical of Hughes: irony, fragments for pictures, exclamations in exposition, contrasts, ambiguities, and paradoxes. Not everywhere is the style felicitous. Some dialogue in gaining brevity loses realism; the several uses of "terribly" and "awfully" are dated; and a few fresh metaphors grow stale through repetition. But the ambiguity is often finely drawn: Arnie, pouting and stubborn, goes to bed "feeling very black"; and Emily, shaken by Arnie's approach to the table with Vivi, rises "white" from her seat. Some contrasts are tellingly wrought: the long hymns chanted from Mapleton's "stiff pews" set against the gay tunes floating from Claudina's apartment, and the "poor little Arnie" of New England versus the "black devil" and "black fool" of Paris. Hughes thoughtfully places his only mordant criticism of American democracy in the mouth of a refractory adolescent bent on hurting the woman who unsatisfactorily replaced his mother, and reserves for the peak of Arnie's outburst the boy's pathetic defense that his father was a fool to die fighting in the Argonne.

"Poor Little Black Fellow" stands out, among these three stories, for its complex of subtle themes. Its nondramatic first half is relieved by controlled and often picturesque irony. More attention to music in Arnie's personal history, however, would have provided the link to Vivi that his appreciation of lovely dresses provides to Claudina. This sincere tale steadily conveys its central point—that Negroes, even little ones, want only to be treated like everyone else.

3. *"Rejuvenation Through Joy"*

The remaining story, "Rejuvenation Through Joy," already being considered for moving-picture production by March, 1934, was probably written in January.[3] Unpublished until the 1934 collection, it reappeared three years later in Dorothy Brewster's *A Book of Contemporary Short Stories*. Speaking in September, 1960, of its background, Hughes said: "There was the Great Om in the 1920's in Westchester County, who charged about one hundred dollars per day for [treatment] that involved lavish entertainment. I took that and I had the entertainment be a jazz band." Using a cult that availed itself, Hughes remarked the following July, of "a place like a deluxe summer hotel," he opens his story with handsome, suave Eugene Lesche lecturing on "Motion and Joy" in a New York hotel. Over a thousand pairs of arms, mostly feminine, reach for the sun at his command. The listeners, caught in this mass tropism and swaying like trees, are told that their "life-centers," too often immobilized in chairs, should be pointed more nearly at the sun. Watch Negroes, advises Lesche, for they "in their natural states, *never* sit in chairs" but live through movement, music, and joy. A month later, the Westchester Colony of Joy opens.

In a long flashback, the reader learns that Lesche rose from circus-chariot rider, art model, and swimming instructor to a profitable alliance with gym-owner Sol Blum, with whom he saw in Paris a wealthy former lady friend of his own eager to spend lavishly at a "happiness" colony near Digne. Hurrying back to New York, the two men combine the rage for Negro jazz and the fad of soul colonies into the union "black rhythm and happy souls." A Yale dropout whom they hire to study primitive art, jazz, eurhythmy, and Freud writes twenty-minute lectures for Lesche, who brushes up on the latest Harlem jazz steps. Sol ironically orients the Negro band and Tulane Lucas, "the blues-singing little coal-black dancer," about the religious and thera-peutic functions of the colony. Tap dancers and Miss Lucas, with "plenty of hip movement," are to teach the bored, rich members how to use their life-centers.

The winter after the colony has lured "all the smart neuras-thenics from Park Avenue," the staff and members adopt such titles as New Man, New Woman, and Earth-Drummer. Another innovation is New Leader Lesche's Private Hours, which run so irregularly one afternoon that New Woman Althouse throws an African stool at her leader for consulting at too great length with New Woman Reeves. The following spring is too joyful to be adequately shared with Lesche by all devotees. Some New Ones stop speaking to one another, and the colony attracts newspaper-men, blackmailers, and other racketeers.

The Colony of Joy collapses the morning the Earth-Drummer, supposedly sharing the excesses of spring with Tulane Lucas, drives up from a night in the city just in time to take his place in the band at Lesche's morning lecture. He is immediately dis-lodged by a pistol shot from the palm trees as Miss Lucas's bullet strikes "somewhere near his life-center." Lesche himself has to step briskly in the subsequent disorder. "As a final touch," adds the author, "one of the tabloids claimed to have discovered that the great Lesche was a Negro—passing for white!"

This diverting third-person story handles a colorful offshoot of the cult theme. The misinformation about Harlemites that flows from the Yale man's pen and from Lesche's lips filches checks from people east of Fifth Avenue; but it deprives no one of his individuality, at least within the world of the story. Lesche's tomfoolery about Negroes' never sitting in chairs is harmless, but his claim that they know only joy has a minstrel-man source. The passages in which Hughes exposes the cult, both in Sol's lecture to the "curative" Negro band and in its rehearsal, are ironic: "This will not be no night club. Nor will it be a dance hall. This place is more like a church. It's for the rebuilding of souls—and bodies. It's for helping people . . . sick and bored, *ennui-ed* in other words . . . come here for . . . real primitive jazz out of Africa (you know, Harlem) to help 'em learn to move, to walk, to live. . . ."

Then, rehearsing, wearing red—"the color of joy"—the "primitive" band plays for background Duke Ellington's *Mood Indigo*. To the syncopated moan, bushy-haired Miss Lucas dances out with instructive undulations, while Lesche says in a soft voice, prompted by the Yale man: "*See how the Negroes live, dark as the earth, the primitive earth, swaying like trees, rooted in the deepest source of life.* Then I'm gonna have 'em all rise and sway, like Miss Lucas here. That ought to keep 'em from being bored until lunch time." Sol, watching Miss Lucas's contortions, exclaims, "Goddam! It's worth the money!" After the hip-shaker's "Hey! Hey!" Lesche restrains them with a "Sh-ss-ss-s! Be dignified."

Whereas the story of Arnie mixes cult and cant, this one mixes cult and confusion—a confusion existent after the stock market crash. Wealthy followers of this confidence-man, looking back on an exuberant decade of fads (Mah Jong, cross-word puzzles, and marathon dancing), heroes (Bobby Jones, Red Grange, Rudolph Valentino, and "Lucky Lindy"), and various sensations (the Leopold-Loeb, Scopes, and Sacco-Vanzetti trials, and popular versions of Freud, Adler, and Jung), now seek fresh revelations. Lesche's female adorers reflect American women of the early 1930's who, doing a right-face from short skirts, bobbed hair, and "red-hot baby" mannerisms, were ready for the comforts of soul-saving.

This story, then, evokes the feel and attitudes of several years of the American past, and of socially important people who were idle, silly, or neurotic. Referring to criticisms of the Colony of Joy, Hughes mentions in the story the magazines that sent disturbing eddies through the stream of American thought, *The Nation* and *The Forum*—allowing the green-covered *American Mercury* to hover unnamed in the background. In the background too are names that would be more strongly connotative to readers in 1934: Gurdjieff, Russian mystic who in the late

1920's counselled inner observation and silent concentration at Fontainebleau; Gilbert Seldes, whose adaptation of the sexually daring *Lysistrata* was contemporaneous with the Colony of Joy; and Jean Harlow, blonde exemplar of sex and beauty to cinema fans of the 1930's.

The fact that this story attracted both theatrical and moving-picture producers indicates its varieties of appeal. Most of its overt humor—less artful than the consistent, half-smile wit that carries the tale—has a touch of the ridiculous. For example, Mrs. Ken Prather, II, spends "months entire kneeling holding her big toes behind her, deep in contemplation." Mr. Jones, the fan painter, changes his name to Horse; but at summer's end he is "even less of a horse than before." The African stools, good for either contemplating or brawling, rather humorously and iron-ically tie a faint knot of theme and action. And humor mixes with excellent word order as Hughes tells of the jealous Mrs. Althouse, who threatens "to ring at once the Baroness' neck." No penetration of character or serious action appears in the tale. Cheerful hoax pervades it; and readers may find themselves wishing Lesche a businessman's success, giving in to that attitude which Phineas T. Barnum over a century ago found character-istic of his countrymen.

A comparison between Hughes's illumination of the cult of the Negro in his poems and in his stories can be misleading, just as the physical impressiveness of the sixteen-line "Minstrel Man" can seem unfairly pitted against the bulk of the twenty-six-page "Poor Little Black Fellow." This surface inequality of the two genres, as understood outside the realm of literature, is as obvious as the fact that a few jewels and a few boulders might assay the same value; but the fingertips would handle the one and the hands and arms be applied to the other. In literature the case is not so clear. But to every reader who has been moved to mem-orize certain poems while he has almost completely forgotten certain stories, the spatial imbalance in the treatment of the two genres suggests no comparative value.

This defense of the slenderness of poetry is not weakened by the observation that Hughes's stories do more and better work than his poems in dissecting the cult of the Negro. "Slave on the Block" and "Minstrel Man" are equally vivid incisions of a falsely conceived portrait. "Theme for English B" and "Aesthete in Harlem" complement some of the Pemberton attitudes toward

Arnie and Negroes in general. The other two poems are minor, independent echoes of themes more emphatically and artistically woven into the stories.

Hughes's best commentary on this theme, then, is found in "Poor Little Black Fellow," "Slave on the Block," and "Minstrel Man." All deserve to be remembered—the stories for their bright and complex probing of the nation's most insidious cult; the poem for its poignant display of the nation's oldest mannikin.

CHAPTER **3**

The Face of Prejudice

That wasn't no Santa Claus
. . . he's just a old white man.
—*One Christmas Eve*

I N A SEPTEMBER, 1960, INTERVIEW, to a question about his literary aims, Hughes replied, "I explain and illuminate the Negro condition in America. This applies to 90 percent of my work." A perfect fulfillment of that aim might not impress a few corners of the American audience. In 1958, for example, a contributor to a survey of contemporary belles-lettres wrote that "very little remains to be said" about American racial discrimination, while a book reviewer for *The New York Times* (November 2, 1958) was asserting that "there is very little that has not been said about [apartheid in] Africa." But another critic's observation, published within a week or so of Hughes's declaration, was that "few, if any, literary universes are as impoverished as the universe of Negro fiction," which treats mainly the ghetto, "the fundamental fact of life for Negroes," presided over by "the ogre of an irony . . . bound up with American color caste. . . ."[1]

From these statements the suggestion arises that writing about racial prejudice in America is like either taking corn to Iowa or setting an extra empty plate on a poor man's table. The nature of man is not so happily disposed that he feels bound to examine equally the many forms that truth may assume. But the function of the student of letters is to open his shop to every authentic form of printed life, to the end that the inconsequential may be thoughtfully proved so, and the conceivably vital preserved for better judgments.

As a high school senior, Hughes had left imitation of Dunbar's dialect poems. His early ethnic sympathies had been sharpened by the headstrong rancor of his father and then richly broadened by his absorption into the crowded Negro communities of Harlem and Washington. As he moved unavoidably toward the theme of racial prejudice, his sensitivity was fated to collide with the walls of Negrophobia and separatism.

I *Porters, Sharecroppers, and Pretty Girls*

At nineteen, having come to New York from Mexico, Hughes was painfully aware of his "first positive feeling that Negro emancipation was not progressing well." This feeling, he told an audience at Monterey Peninsula College in 1958, impelled him to write "Elevator Boy,"[2] perhaps his earliest verse to decry economic discrimination. The more popular "Porter" has more economy of phrase; expressing the same resentment, it has the sharpness—helped by sibilants—of covertly tossed scorn; and it ends with the jut-of-the-lip surliness appropriate to muttered sarcasm: "Rich old white man/Owns the world./Gimme yo' shoes/To shine./Yes, sir!"

Considering the pervasiveness of economic prejudice against Negroes, and Hughes's reputation for keeping his finger on the Negro pulse, it is not surprising that his poetry comments at least twice as often on economic abuse as on any other kind. Although most of his strictures aim at urban communities, some criticize the rural South. "Share Croppers" thus concludes its picture of field workers, hungry, unpaid, no more "Than a herd of Negroes/Driven to the field—/Plowing life away/To make the cotton yield."

A singular but largely unspoken hazard faced by many pretty colored girls in the South is scored in "Ruby Brown," a poem Hughes wrote when he was about twenty-one. Beautiful Ruby, for whom the town of Mayville has no place "Nor fuel for the clean flame of joy/That tried to burn within her soul," is pressed by educational and job discrimination into a stingy old white woman's kitchen. Because of an unrecognized need for joy, Ruby ends up in "the sinister shuttered houses of the bottoms" where white men pay her more than they ever did in their kitchens.

Almost fifteen years later, a shade of Ruby Brown wrought some financial havoc in Hughes's life. His second autobiography records how his mother's generosity to her young and pretty distant cousin consumed several months' expense money that

Hughes had deposited in support of her and his half-brother before leaving for Spain. "Ruby Brown" is recalled by the fact that the young beauty of 1937, a recent high-school graduate, left a Southern home town that had no jobs for Negro girls. She was pregnant.

A similarly oriented poem, "Red Silk Stockings," raised a squall of condemnation from the best-foot-forward school of Negro book reviewers. They were startled and ashamed to see in *Fine Clothes to the Jew* this advice for an attractive Negro girl in the rural South:

> Go out and let the white boys
> Look at yo' legs.
>
> Ain't nothin' to do for you, nohow,
> Round this town—
> You's too pretty.
> Put on yo' red silk stockings, gal. . . .

The Pittsburgh Courier, which had headlined the volume as "trash," invited the student poet to defend himself. Hughes did so on April 16, 1927, in a nine-point rejoinder entitled "These Bad Negroes: A Critique on Critics." The second, third, and fourth points read thus:

> My poems are indelicate. But so is life.
> I write about "harlots and gin-bibers." But they are human. Solomon, Homer, Shakespeare, and Walt Whitman were not afraid or ashamed to include them.
> "Red Silk Stockings." An ironical poem deploring the fact that in certain Southern rural communities there is little work for a beautiful colored girl to do other than the selling of her body—a fact for one to weep over rather than disdain to recognize.

The themes of these five poems also deeply mark some of Hughes's stories. "Berry," in his first collection, develops, according to the author's own statement in September, 1960, "the fact that often Negro servants are looked up to for their joy of living, especially by the white children." Recalling his own youth, no doubt, and speaking of employment offices that sent out servants not described beforehand as Negro to prospective employers, he declared in July, 1961: "Agencies would take your money and send you on any job, and the people would look at you as if you were crazy."

The story, first printed in *Abbott's Weekly* early in 1934, opens with similar astonishment on the part of Mrs. Osborn, a housekeeper at Dr. Renfield's Summer Home for Crippled Children, when Jersey City's High Class Help Agency sends her a kitchen boy. Not daring to lodge Milberry Jones with the "handyman-gardener-chauffeur," she hurries with her race problem to Dr. Renfield, to whom rumor ties her affections. The doctor, hearing that Milberry's Scandinavian predecessor had received ten dollars weekly, says, "Well, pay the darkie eight."

Milberry must rise at five-thirty to do the extra jobs foisted upon him by the handyman, the waitresses, and the housekeeper. He concludes that practically everything about the place is sham except the crippled children "there like himself because they couldn't help it." Called one day to help get the excited cripples to the beach, Berry (as they now call him) unavoidably lets a too eager boy fall to the lawn. The staff, fearing bad publicity, judges Berry "criminally careless." The child, who kicks at Dr. Renfield when he tries to take him out of Berry's arms for examination, is unhurt. Deducting a week's pay for the broken chair, the doctor discharges Berry, who must return to Jersey City, where he has just endured weeks of hunger.

Prejudice is sometimes elusive and deep, but no individual receives special censure. At the outset, Mrs. Osborn defers to the assumed tastes of a handyman who is allowed, like several staff members, to transfer tasks to one who can object only by risking his job. The whites as a group are selfish, gossipy, and mean-spirited, granting what seems a privilege only when they can thereby evade a responsibility. They childishly show their prejudices by remarks about Berry's darkness, by feigned Southern accents and mispronounced words—deriding the boy for not having the education withheld from him by his native Georgia. Dr. Renfield, himself a faker who self-consciously employs his "movie beard" and feminine eyes, schemes to defraud crippled children. As omniscient author, Hughes's most subtle stroke accompanies the dismissal of Berry, when Dr. Renfield orders that he pay ten dollars for the broken chair. The housekeeper has to remind him that "we don't pay him but eight." The doctor, like the rest of the staff, whose impositions upon Berry have become routine, is no longer conscious of his discrimination.

II Carousels and Christmas: The Young Ones

Hughes's concern over the effect of prejudice on children, implicit in "Berry," is emphatic elsewhere. His often-published and widely translated poem "Merry-Go-Round," first printed in 1942, pictures the confusion of a migrant Southern Negro child who cannot decide, at a carnival, which horse to mount. Accustomed to back-seat Jim Crow rules on trains and buses, she says: "But there ain't no back/To a merry-go-round!/Where's the horse/For a kid that's black?" The turnabout here is social and psychological, as well as mechanical. One sees the surprise of structure falling apart, the pathos of innocence assembling tainted pieces. This poem, resting its case simply and almost entirely on its perfect idea, seems one of those rare works that flow quickly and evenly from the mind.

An updated companion-piece to "Merry-Go-Round" is "Children's Rhymes," in *Montage of a Dream Deferred* (1951). In this poem slum children chant: "By what sends/the white kids/I ain't sent:/I know I can't/be President." Another rhyme asserts: "What's written down/for white folks/ain't for us a-tall:/'Liberty And Justice—/Huh—For All.'" The tough-skinned surface of these ditties and their hopscotch rhythm hide some of the bitterness from the reader, just as the sidewalk games absorb the realizations of the children.

The story that most obviously treats prejudice against the young was written in January, 1939, as "Inside Us"[3] and was published in 1941 in *The Crisis* as "One Friday Morning." Nancy Lee Johnson, a popular high-school senior, easily wins the annual art scholarship, only to be summoned by the assistant principal to hear a nice letter explaining why the Artist Club does not "feel it would be fair" to accept her as winner. The words "liberty and justice for all" clog Nancy's throat as she remembers her planned acceptance speech (in contrast to the slum urchins who snap up new phrases for gutterside games). Nancy recovers by Friday morning assembly time, but she salutes the flag with tears in her eyes. Although Hughes considers this narrative (which recalls Clara Dieke, his art teacher at Central High) his most contrived story, its final emphasis on both racial and American pride as surmounters of prejudice explains its appearance in anthologies.

The autobiographical strain is more substantial in "One Christ-mas Eve." The author spoke in September, 1960, of its source as being his "own childhood experience with a Santa Claus who didn't pay any attention to Negro children." Written in Carmel in November, 1933, and published in *Opportunity* the following month,[4] this story tells of the colored maid, Arcie, and her little boy, Joe. Paid only part of her small wages by her white Maryland employers on Christmas Eve, Arcie has Joe wait out-side the dime store in the snow, so that his gift will surprise him. Joe surprises his mother, instead, by disappearing; he is attracted by a Santa Claus giving children presents in a motion-picture theater lobby. But the children are white; and little Joe learns a lesson—through a loud tin-pan rattle fiercely shaken in his face by Santa, and through the laughter that pursues him into the street filled with more white people. What he learns is made clear at the end of the story by his worried mother, who shakes him hard with her free hand:

> "Huh! That wasn't no Santa Claus," Arcie explained. "If it was, he wouldn't a-treated you like that. That's a theatre for white folks—I told you once—and he's just a old white man."
> "Oh," said little Joe.

In this story, one sees the face of prejudice slowly emerge, pro-tean and amorphous. It is as familiar as one's employer, as in-nocuous as a laughing child, as kindly as Santa Claus. Yet, it is none of these. Arcie recognizes it by massing her employers namelessly in what she sees as a "darned inconsiderate" fraternity simply called white folks. Hughes turns these white faces from the reader, but symbolically they are in the snow, which makes Arcie aware of her worn-out shoes, and which is cold but nice for the holidays. They are in the "white" motion-picture lobby only fleetingly and illusively warm for a Negro child. White people, and Santa himself, become as unreal to little Joe as the tinsel snow he sees on the jolly man's beard. To him and his mother, a Santa who has a face like a white man is no Santa at all.

Joe cannot read the signs in the lobby that greet "patrons" and "customers." All the white people grin, sensing the incon-gruity. The Christmas-time crowd is not consciously unfriendly as it scares the child, with a gale of laughter, into a white street with new faces more meaningful to him than ever.

Hughes tells the story simply, with unsentimentalized pathos, and without sacrificing symbolic penetration and his usual irony.

III Jim Crow in Public

Unlike holidays that only briefly affect attitudinal environments, governmental and community operations are of momentous daily importance. A number of Hughes's works comment on how Negroes are burdened by prejudiced administration of government and in housing. Four poems are representative in their barely mediocre artistry but faithful presentation of the worst material feature of slum life: "Madam and the Rent Man," "Ballad of the Landlord," "Visitors to the Black Belt," and "Restrictive Covenants," all collected in volumes between 1942 and 1951. Two stanzas from "Madam and the Rent Man" (*Poetry*, September, 1943) indicate the general content of these poems:

> The sink is broke,
> The water don't run,
> And you ain't done a thing
> You promised to've done.

> Back window's cracked,
> Kitchen floor squeaks,
> There's rats in the cellar.
> And the attic leaks.

"Restrictive Covenants" (*One-Way Ticket* [1949]) opens with a few verses on what is probably the third most important fact in the life of an American Negro: "When I move/Into a neighborhood/Folks fly." Entire books, such as Robert Weaver's *The Negro Ghetto*, have been required to trace the ramifications of those verses into the most powerful economic and social institutions of the nation. Upstart civic and parent organizations defending neighborhood schools and housing discrimination have crowded the records of the 1950's and 1960's with distortions of the fact behind this technically inconsequential poem.

In one of his favorite stories, Hughes treats a peculiarly onerous kind of government-tolerated prejudice: that suffered by Negro military men. The background of "Sailor Ashore," the author said, "is more or less my merchant marine days." He elaborated, in July, 1961: "This grew out of the last paragraph in the story: 'If I ever *did* have a son . . . I'd make something out of my son. . . .' I overheard this in a Los Angeles bar—a hopeless statement like this, since it looked as if the man wouldn't likely have a son. I took that sentence or so and went home that night and wrote the story—or it was very soon afterwards. It seemed to me so sad, you know." "Sailor Ashore," written in 1941 at Hollow Hills Farm[5] and published in *Laughing to Keep from Crying*, tells of the flirtation between a sailor named Bill and a streetwalker named Azora. Their repartee, known to jazz insiders as "hepcat rhymed jive," easily leads, with the aid of bootleg whiskey and mutual candidness, to Azora's room.

Questioned about his sad-eyed examination of his liquor glass, Bill says he is trying to see his "black future" and informs the questioner that hers will have a similar hue. Azora dissents, claiming an eleven-year-old son for whom she has bright plans. The ensuing discussion covers prejudice in the navy and at the Los Angeles port, lynchings, and wartime nostrums about liberty. When Azora questions the manliness of his gloomy outlook, Bill departs. But Azora calls him back, confesses that she has no son and is "nothing but a hustler." Told by Bill that he has known it all along, she flings back: " 'Yeah? Well, listen, kid! If I ever *did* have a son—and if I ever do have a job—if I wasn't what I am—I'd make something out of my son, if I had one! I swear to God I would, sailor!' "

In this story, ending at its emotional peak, Hughes as omniscient author says much about how prejudice corrodes character. Unlike the men of the West Illana Series, Bill is a sailor without passion or vigor. Given to sudden lapses into wordless inertia, he is thinned out and passive before a hostile environment. The stripes on his arm give him no feeling of substance as a servant of his country. He feels caged in "a white man's world," where talk of one's son, the next generation, merely heats the irony of one's own predicament. He cannot think of manhood as a consuming struggle to secure conditions long taken for granted by his shipmates. "If things is bad," chides Azora, "change 'em! You a man, ain't you?" But her advice is to him the "hard" solution, for he evades her with "You a mighty hard chick to get along with."

Hughes gives the reader the task of fitting the sailor's spiritual bog into the democratic landscape. He balances Bill against Chicago-born Azora, who is not a clear product of discrimination: she is not another Ruby Brown or girl with red silk stockings. But her lies belong to the milieu into which the prejudice of the

Los Angeles port, whose bars refuse to serve Negroes, forces Bill while "on liberty" from naval duties. Through two of Azora's remarks, Hughes throws ambiguity over her advice and character. "Boy," she reprimands, "you talk like you just now finding out you're colored." A moment later she says of bigoted whites, "But I can deal with 'em, can't you?" Here she supports extensive compromise as apparently compatible with the aggressive manliness she urges.

Hughes shows the weight of prejudice as deadening even to the atmosphere of commercialized love. He suggests this perverse ability through contrasts: flirtatious, slangy dalliance opposed to gloomy pessimism, whiskey and easy morality opposed to a desperate lie. Azora's possible motives for telling that lie and for recanting in a voice "harder than before"—neither act being relevant to her trade—add complexity to Hughes's method of imbuing his characters with humanity.

The author's poetry reveals related forms of public discrimination. "Ballad of the Landlord" censures prejudice in courts of law. "Parade" mirrors a faintly humorous type of police discrimination still in actual practice: the enforced speed-up by motorcycle or other police escorts of parades and similar demonstrations that display Negro unity. The most grievous form of public discrimination, inequality of opportunity in education, touched only lightly in his poetry (as in "Theme for English B"), wholly informs "Professor." This story, completed by November, 1934, and published in *The Anvil* for May-June, 1935, as "Dr. Brown's Decision,"[6] appeared in Dorothy Brewster's *A Book of Contemporary Short Stories* in 1936. Hughes said the story reflects "common incidents in the educational field." He added in July, 1961, that it is based "on a number of college deans and presidents I've known who had to compromise their own integrity to get money for their schools." He might have added his own experience at Lincoln University, where a famous old alumnus criticized Hughes's survey of racial attitudes on the campus, a report written for a sociology course. The facts of the survey were true, the old educator conceded; but he reminded Hughes that he could never have built his big Middle Western institution by telling the truth to whites. He implied, Hughes writes in *The Big Sea*, that cooperation from them could be secured only by "flattery, cajolery, good-natured begging, lying, and general Uncle Toming—not by truth."

As "Professor," a story narrated in the third person, opens, colored Dr. T. Walton Brown is picked up by a deferential white chauffeur and driven from the ghetto-bound Booker T. Washington Hotel to the beautiful home of philanthropist Ralph P. Chandler. A dinner guest, along with Dr. Bulwick of the local (border state) municipal college, Dr. Brown moves from courteous remarks about Negro progress to a discussion of his conservative *The Sociology of Prejudice*. That book, he finds, has converted his present fund-raising lecture tour into an opportunity to secure the financial blessings of Mr. Chandler and his ever-smiling wife, who, at the moment, is asking whether he does not think "*your* people are happier in schools of their own." After pointing out that his own degree was unobtainable in a Negro school, Dr. Brown snaps into the required diplomatic posture with "You are right" when the thought of his mission ends his memory of ghettoes and Jim Crow. The seal is affixed when Dr. Bulwick, whose college refuses to admit Negroes, sanctions Dr. Brown's book in its dependence on Christian fellowship, whereupon Mrs. Chandler says, "How beautiful."

Mr. Chandler, purse strings thus loosened, asks Dr. Brown how much his college—"university, I believe you call it," is his polite correction needs for first class improvement. The figures, readily forthcoming, appear as "sane and conservative" to the Chandlers as the book; and, in the mellow spirit of this confidence, they abandon thoughts of building a junior college for Negroes in their town. They will turn such applicants southward, toward "a professor of their own race." Over coffee, the talk turns to the coming theatrical season and to Mrs. Chandler's love for Negro singers. Aware of his hosts' delight, Dr. Brown speeds luxuriously back to the Booker T. Washington, thinking: ". . . with six thousand dollars a year [for an endowed chair of sociology] earned by dancing properly to the tune of Jim Crow education, he could carry his whole family to South America for a summer where they wouldn't need to feel like Negroes."

Educational prejudice is Hughes's main concern in this large picture. Dr. Brown, rejected by decent hotels, is pressed into quarters where stealthily procured prostitutes and cheap whiskey mean more than hot water and good service. Driven partly by shame into the lobby to wait for the chauffeur, he feels unsafe in the luxurious car because he is almost in the South. Eating a sumptuous dinner, he must tell polite lies about Negroes and listen to his hostess's genial pretenses about the happiness with which segregation supposedly enhances their plight. Bowing to Mr. Chandler's wealth, Dr. Brown balances the poor education (and chances for staff research) backed by semi-Southern money against the thorough discrimination that an even poorer education would entrench.

Hughes's irony shows in the white professor's telling the colored one that he has found some educated Negroes "most intelligent." It appears amusingly in Mrs. Chandler's affection for colored singers and painfully in Dr. Brown's sense that his hosts have been delighted by a compromise oppressive to Negroes. The symbol used by the author appears, uncharacteristically, in a person, Booker T. Washington. In his earlier novel, *Not Without Laughter,* written on the campus where he had received the theory of genuflection from an old practitioner, Hughes used the famous Tuskegee educator as a symbol of conciliation. In "Professor," Dr. Brown must stay in an inferior hotel bearing Washington's name. And the professor's own name has initials that compose an anagram of Washington's.

Hughes presents ambiguities, like the professor's "coming to himself" in agreement with the Chandlers: coming to the time-serving, kowtowing side of himself. Here and there clauses are delicately placed, like the butler's sudden "Dinner is served," which breaks off the facile sanction of segregated education as if it were nonsense. Others have multiple meanings, like "And they bowed farewell," with which the Chandlers and their municipal aide send Dr. Brown back to the ghetto; all are actually bowing to their tradition of discrimination. Hughes employs what amounts to a stream-of-consciousness technique as he delivers a 168-word adjectival modifier of "Dr. Brown" within a single sentence. It wheels before the reader's eyes and Dr. Brown's memory the procession of discriminatory ordeals doggedly borne by the professor in his student days—all obscuring and rendering inconsequential the budgetary figures he is simultaneously giving Mr. Chandler.

Hughes does not admire Dr. Brown, for the views in the professor's book "agreed with the white man's"—yet it is Mr. Chandler's campus representative who draws this conclusion. Hughes is more damaging when he says "Dr. Brown bobbed and bowed," as he practices the gymnastics of an Uncle Tom in the act of surrender and when he exposes the professor's advocacy of "Christian fellowship" as a solution. Hughes probably doubted that religion could be a racial ameliorant. At Hughes's first inter-racial conference, a Y.M.C.A. meeting at Franklin and Marshall College in Pennsylvania in 1928, he had been diverted to Jesus and to prayer when he had proposed to his cordial hosts a resolution that they re-examine their own policy of denying admission to Negro students.

Despite the professor's readiness to tack his fund-raising craft, he has sturdier traits that add the shade of complexity common in Hughes's characters. His determination carried him through two years of remedial study to qualify for a Northern college, and his thousands of nights as a redcap and a waiter add stone to his foundation as a teacher. Whether the author intends such considerations to temper his generally critical attitude toward the professor is conjectural. Certainly he intends no suggestion so uninspired as the notion that living "like a white man," as one reviewer described Dr. Brown's goal, is the *summum bonum* to imaginations of every hue.

This competently written story realistically ends without a resolution of the educational problems. Such a Chekhovian ending shows the continuity of institutionalized prejudice, not at all hindered in its then growing career by its having jostled and engulfed the integrity of one Negro educator.

IV *In the Quarter of the Negroes: A Miscellany*

The Uncle Tom who prompted many of the lines in "Professor" is caught in both private and public stances in Hughes's "Uncle Tom" (*Span*, December, 1944):

> Within—
> The beaten pride.
> Without—
> The grinning face,
> The low, obsequious,
> Double bow,
> The sly and servile grace
> Of one the white folks
> Long ago
> Taught well
> To know his
> Place.

This poem, not deep in meaning and seemingly more revealing than it is, has the evanescence not uncommon to poems that can be read in a single breath. It has the completeness of one low bow, one swing of a revolving door. The form is tailored to the meaning; for Uncle Toms are all curve and surface, and they yield little to close, quick observation.

In other poems, Hughes aims glancing lines at Southern states: in "Bound No'th Blues" (*Opportunity*, October, 1926) Mississippi towns are not "fit for a hoppin' toad." In contrast, "Movies" (*Montage*) shows Harlem laughing at the "crocodile art" of derisive Hollywood. Several poems provide sequels to "Bound No'th Blues" by observing migrants struggling to squeeze themselves into new corners and through new bars in the North. A few stress the flight from Dixie, like the title piece of *One-Way Ticket* (1949) that ends with the migrant "Gone up North,/ Gone out West,/Gone!"

Prejudice does not always stir Hughes to resentful poetic tones. He sometimes turns toward nature, toward innocent forms of life, to suggest that racial discrimination is a hybrid creature of man-made, aberrant principles. "Lullaby (For a Black Mother)," in *The Crisis*, March, 1926, opens, "My little dark baby,/My little earth-thing," and then croons of moon and stars. Near the end, "Oh, little dark baby,/Night black baby" shows black a divine color of cosmic gracefulness. "Restrictive Covenants" comments, more prosaically, that the moon and sun do not flee from Negroes, that the wind does not disdain to blow on Chicago's black South Side. After "Freedom Train" salutes the Negro youngster Jimmy who "died for real" on the Anzio beachhead, it asks for a Freedom Train

> Not stoppin' at no stations marked COLORED nor WHITE,
> Just stoppin' in the fields in the broad daylight,
> Stoppin' in the country in the wide-open air
> Where there never was no Jim Crow signs nowhere. . . .

One of Hughes's best poems, "Dream Variations" (in *Current Opinion*, September, 1924), excellently expresses the unnaturalness of prejudice:

> To fling my arms wide
> In some place of the sun,
> To whirl and to dance
> Till the white day is done.

> Then rest at cool evening
> Beneath a tall tree
> While night comes on gently,
>   Dark like me—
> That is my dream!
>
> To fling my arms wide
> In the face of the sun,
> Dance! Whirl! Whirl!
> Till the quick day is done.
> Rest at pale evening . . .
> A tall, slim tree . . .
> Night coming tenderly
>   Black like me.

This poem rewards close study of its soft poise, its silent pirouette that is almost an ascension. It shows longing, not movement; it means buoyant recoil from long resignation, not primitive exaltation on a literal island of exotic warmth. No extra people belong in this dreamy place of love and relaxation. Through "white day" and "black like me" race enters the poem, making it much more than shimmer and recumbency. In these phrases, sublimated pessimism rises through layers of bigotry, closes the dancer's eyes against human forms, and identifies him with the tenderness of night. "Dream Variations" (from which the middle verse, "That is my dream!", should have been removed) provided the title of John Howard Griffith's *Black Like Me* (1962) and the movie version in 1964, a book relating Griffith's horrifying odyssey through the South disguised as a Negro.

Hughes's usual fairness is evident in his poems on intraracial attitudes. He records an interchange along the rungs of the social ladder in "Low to High" and "High to Low," printed together in *Midwest Journal,* Summer, 1949. The former includes the complaint: "You said you was gonna take me/Up with you —/Now you've got your Cadillac,/you done forgot that you are black." In the latter the reply comes down: "you talk too loud,/cuss too loud,/look too black,/don't get anywhere," followed by reminders of doorstep lounging, shouting in church, and generally "the way you clown—/the way, in other words,/you let me down." The author's whimsical vision of Negro Utopia appears in his unpoetic "Projection" (*Montage*), which glimpses "that day when Abyssinia Baptist Church/throws her enormous arms around/St. James Presbyterian/and 409 Edgecombe/stoops to kiss 12 West 133rd."

Hughes's basic impartiality appears again in his refusal to condemn white people en masse. One of his earliest poems, "The White Ones" (*Opportunity,* March, 1924), declares, "I do not hate you,/. . . Yet why do you torture me?" Twenty-five years later, the mild "Negro Servant" simply shows a Harlemite happy to escape white people after working hours: "O, sweet relief from faces that are white!"

The *One-Way Ticket* that contains "Negro Servant," however, includes poems suggesting the freedom-now attitude that began to transform the 1960's. "Puzzled" is mentionable, like all the poems sketchily quoted here, for its content rather than for its quality; it opens with Harlem "Remembering the old lies,/The old kicks in the back,/The old, *Be patient.*" The same mood runs less concretely through "Democracy," but typically shapes two lines: "I do not need my freedom when I'm dead./I cannot live on tomorrow's bread."

The subterranean rumbling in Negro communities echoed in these poems gives way more often to hopefulness. The popular "I, Too"—"Epilogue" in *The Weary Blues*—has the dinner-time confidence of one who expects handsome armor later on: "They send me to eat in the kitchen/When company comes,/But I laugh,/And eat well,/And grow strong." Five years later "Walkers with the Dawn" and "Song," both in *The Dream Keeper,* show Negroes unafraid, and the latter adds:

> Open wide your arms to life,
> Whirl in the wind of pain and strife,
> Face the wall with the dark closed gate,
> Beat with bare, brown fists—
> And wait.

"Freedom's Plow," Hughes's long wartime poem, patriotically narrates how Negro slaves dreamed and worked to build and spiritualize America. The combination of militancy and hopefulness subserves the national emergency; but the dogged march from slavery to freedom, heralded by a song born of war ("Out of war, it came, bloody and terrible!"), gives real fiber to the poem. The song itself, made up by slaves, gives robustness to the refrain: "Keep your hand on the plow! Hold on!"

The images of wall and fist return in "Dusk" to roughen the air of repose in much of *Fields of Wonder* (1947). The final stanza, after lines about fists beating against a wall, reads: "Walls have been known/To fall,/Dusk turn to dawn,/And chains be gone!"

Hughes does not restrict to these representative poems his understanding of the range of Negroes' responses to prejudice. Two contrasting stories, "Powder-White Faces" and "Something in Common," exemplify the red and the violet in the spectrum. The former story, not autobiographical, evidently appeared in *The Chicago Defender* before its use in *Laughing to Keep from Crying*.[7] It relates the hard times of the Oriental mess-boy Charlie Lee, sailing out of New York as the story opens, twelve hours after having killed a white woman. The rest of the seven-page story lets Charlie lean on the tramp's rail and search his past for an explanation of his deed.

Memory returns him home, to a "little American possession in the Pacific," to English-enforced job discrimination, to "white only" signs hung over beer-garden bars by American marines and accepted by all the girls. At sea, under a changed name, Charlie is jailed after a fight started by Southern rowdies in New Orleans who are unaccustomed to seeing brown men and white women together. He learns about women the hard way: through disease from the rapacious White Russian females of carnival-time Shanghai, through insults and hired-hand beatings arranged by other white women in port-town bars and taxi-dance halls, "women with powder-white faces who took all they could get."

His last job, as houseboy to wealthy Mr. Richards in New York, brings him too close to the man's mistress, who makes suggestive remarks and walks before Charlie in "pink silk things that were only shadows, smiling." She is nice to him, even when he refuses to buy dope for her. Then one dawn after Mr. Richards leaves, she calls Charlie to her silken bed and pulls him down close. He strangles her. Standing at the rail at the close of the story, he understands why: "He did not want her. He only wanted to kill her—this woman who became suddenly *all* white women to him. . . . he smelled . . . the sea into which you can pour all the filth of the world, but the water never gets dirty." This final observation, made in similar language in *The Big Sea*, confirms a theme in the story: the therapeutic value of the sea—one not unlike the tenderness of black night in "Lullaby" and "Dream Variations." The sea initiates Charlie into manhood; gives him peaceful intermissions between hard, poorlv rewarded jobs; and heals his viciously inflicted bruises. And, after the murder, it receives him into its clean wind and unsullied presence with an amoral beneficence.

The effects of prejudice are intestinal: Charlie can "only *feel* why" he has killed. It is cumulative in its disordering of emotions: Charlie relives "the hatred and anger of a lifetime . . . suddenly . . . collected in his heart and gathered in his fingers." It produces irrational generalizing: he knows this woman has "really done nothing to him. Not *this* woman." And, like the iron bars of the New Orleans jail, it injures not only the body but "his soul . . . too"; it hurts with wounds beyond the sanative powers of the ocean.

These features of prejudice are made feminine, specific in remembered abuses, general in the comfort turned sour and repulsive; and they gather loosely in the nameless dope addict whose caress is tragic. Hughes names emotions that spread through Charlie: anger, loathing, fear, hatred, distrust, contempt, suspicion—all spawned by long discrimination that poisons the girl's last words, "You're a cute China boy! Kiss me." Hughes's recognition of universal suffering directs his choice of an Oriental protagonist, and he decides that not all of Charlie's misfortunes must bespeak prejudice. The White Russian girls are driven by hunger and greed that play no favorites, and a New York blonde who finds his weekly salary insufficient heeds a universal urge. But the tale is slightly repetitious, although it succeeds in giving a picture of the chaos that prejudice can bring swelling into the individual mind. It became the title piece of *Weissgepuderte Gesichter* (1961), a German collection of ten of Hughes's stories.

"Something in Common," which also has no concrete source in Hughes's experience, simply shows the fact, he said in July, 1961, that "American Negroes abroad become much more patriotic than they are at home, especially if they hear talk from a white person." The story, first published in *The Chicago Defender* on March 17, 1934,[8] opens in a Hong Kong bar where two elderly derelicts, one colored and one white, become acquainted. They exchange names and a bit of personal history, the white man revealing less. When the Kentucky colonel and the Missouri Negro exchange views on women and on America, conflict leads to insults and threats of fisticuffs as the two old men "square off like roosters, rocking a little from age and gin . . . gnarled fists doubled up." The British bartender throws them into the street before either can strike a blow. Incensed at this man who has "no rights to put his Cockney hands on Americans," they stagger back into the bar, arm in arm, "to protect their honor against the British."

The humor and irony in this rather farcical sketch soften the lineaments of prejudice, carried shabbily into Hong Kong by Colonel McBride, who cannot detect some of the Negro's sarcasm. McBride's calling his companion "boy" and "George" also takes on the lightness of banter. As each man competitively praises women of his own race, the white man considers himself lessening the Negro's claim to mulatto beauties by pointing out that "half of 'em has white pappys"—thus exposing one of America's grossest hypocrisies. Other subtle but indelible marks of the colonel's attitude are his arrogance hidden in bluffness, his ready intrusion into his companion's personal affairs, and his withholding his first name. In comparison, the violent name-calling is meaningless. Slight and anecdotal alongside "Powder-White Faces," the sketch is thematically secure in its revelations of the color line.

An anecdote was the actual source of "Tain't So," written in Oberlin in September, 1935,[9] and first published in *Fight* the following year. "There was no Negro in the joke," Hughes said in September, 1960. "I changed it to a Negro; that would make the white woman madder than ever." The angered woman is the ailing, Alabama-born Lucy Cannon, who hobbles to a Pasadena faith healer, only to find that the famous woman is a Negro who irritatingly says "Tain't so" to every complaint. The angry woman bounces out, "walking like the wind"; then she discovers that for the first time in three years she needs no cane.

The author's satire is befittingly mild, such as the reflections of the fainting spells and social agitations of Southern belles. Barbs aimed at prejudice are hardly sharper: Miss Cannon feels "horror" as a big, dark colored woman dares to enter the front door and sit down; and, forgetting her good breeding, she screams at the trespassing proprietress. The excellence she finally concedes to the faith healer she explains as the "supernatural con-

juring powers" of Negroes. But she turns grim at the end of the
story: " 'But the impudence of 'em! Soon's they get up North—
calling herself *Miss* Pauline Jones . . . and charging me Ten
Dollars for a handful of Tain't so's!' "

The last story plays the theme of prejudice to a rhumba beat.
"Spanish Blood" is a purely fictitious narrative, Hughes said in
July, 1961, except for the breaking up of the night club in which
"Duke Ellington or somebody was to open" in the 1930's. Emerson Harper's comment, differing slightly from his nephew's,
placed the event in the 1920's: "In the 1920's there were a bunch
of night clubs along Lenox and Seventh Avenues: the Cotton
Club, Atlantic Club, Connie's Inn. Nearby, there was a new
club, with fine hardwood floors, drapes, mirrors, ready to open.
But mobsters, guys like Dutch Schultz, Vincent Coll, and others
couldn't agree on who was to exercise control, so they sent men
in with axes. They tore up drapes, ruined the floor with axes."[10]

"Spanish Blood," written probably in Carmel and put in final
form by October, 1934,[11] was published in *Metropolis* (December 29, 1934) and in *Stag* (August, 1937) before its appearance
in *Laughing to Keep from Crying*. The story is about handsome
Valerio Gutierrez, son of a Puerto Rican sailor and a Harlem
laundress. Valerio is a rhumba dancer in Harlem who could "do
it in the real Cuban way that made all the girls afraid to dance
with him." His dancing makes him prince of the night-life circle
until a famous blonde dancer gives him a big, red roadster—
out of money she regularly receives from the king of the
champagne racket. Policemen pocket bribes from Valerio's
partner, but still join "five Italian gentlemen in evening clothes"
when they apply the axes, and their own rosewood clubs show
a predilection for Negroes. Valerio, his "lesson" traced on his
face in a long billy scar, leaves for Brazil to dance more rhumbas.

This relatively light-hearted, third-person story merges the
themes of prejudice and the cult of the Negro, with emphasis on
a figure individualized in Hughes's works: the Negro mother.
While whites who are enthralled at becoming "real Harlem initiates" follow Valerio home to stare at his dancing and to try
awkward steps of their own, Valerio's distrustful mother Hattie
sticks to the Chinese laundry. She becomes symbolically the dark
American consciously turning from whites to selfhood in the heart
of black Harlem: she trusts nothing but unending struggle—not

as a domestic serving whites, but as a laborer in the heat of a Chinese laundry. Hughes's repetition of her dogged trust intensifies her meaning.

Vivid passages brighten an already lively style, some advancing the minor theme of intraracial color bias, some showing the physical dash and vivacity that nerved the flow of Manhattan tourists during the Harlem Renaissance. The rhumba beat gives undulation to the theme of the "good-timer," the young man who sleeps all day, carouses all night, and with careless generosity shares his earnings or pawns his suit. The reader gets brief but sure images of the gangster-ridden 1920's, as well as a doorway peep at the glamor of Harlem's Sugar Hill.

Hughes, in imaginatively expressing the many features of prejudice, exhibits the range of merit usual in his poetry and fiction. His most representative works trace the byways of this large theme. His reputation as the writer whose ear is the most harmoniously tuned to reverberations in the Negro quarter is confirmed in the substantial agreement between his emphases and those found in representative public expressions of Negroes. Discrimination in education, employment, and housing, for example, has for years been stressed by Negroes as their fundamental deprivation. White hostility to intermarriage is at the very bottom of the list of Negroes' grievances, and Hughes almost never mentions it. The miracle of American history is the steadfast hopefulness of the Negro people, despite the incredible inhumanity displayed toward them. Hughes again and again returns to this optimistic theme in poetry and prose.

Hughes, then, moves full circle in content and comes near the upper and lower limits of his artistic power in these stories and poems. Most of his best poems and stories treat other themes, but his works aimed at prejudice bring light to some of the obscure portals of the American consciousness. The poems vary qualitatively more than the stories. As a group they are comprehensive, treating fifteen or more distinct kinds of prejudice; but their average technical quality is mediocre, and some are quite like prose. The group includes several popular poems, as well as one ("Red Silk Stockings") that roused a crosswind of notoriety athwart Hughes's early climb to fame. Set highest among them is "Dream Variations," a calm spin of beauty in the act of withdrawal and quiet ascension. Out of eleven stories devoted pri-

marily to this theme,[12] none is dull or awkward. "Trouble with
the Angels," not discussed here, is the most factual in origin and
treatment. "Tain't So" and "Something in Common" are the
slightest, and "Professor" is the most abundantly meaningful and
controlled.

All these stories show varying combinations of mentality, attitudes, beliefs, and moods that issue from prejudice, which itself
is shown as individual and yet deceptively changing in its
features. It is stern with authority and distant with anonymity
in "One Friday Morning." It is selfish, preoccupied, and vindictive
in "Berry." It has the iron lines of old tradition in "African
Morning," the other story not discussed. In "One Christmas Eve"
it has gay, holiday eyes that laugh Santa Claus all the way out
of a little boy's world. In "Powder-White Faces" it has a diseased
smile and a round of artifices for turning pretty graces into
taunts. In "Sailor Ashore" it tells lies through the lips of its own
victim. It is ludicrous with outdated postures in "Tain't So" and
enfeebled by an outworn votary in "Something in Common." It is
dignified in "Professor" by elegance and reputation; sanctified
in "Trouble with the Angels" by a well-rehearsed god. In "Spanish
Blood" it scowls behind an axe and tarnishes a silver badge with
its name. Prejudice is all of these, more simple and more complex.
It is susceptible of more extenuation, yet deserving of even more
infamy than Hughes gives it in these poems and stories.

CHAPTER 4

The Christ and the Killers

Way Down South in Dixie
(Bruised body high in air)
I asked the white Lord Jesus
What was the use of prayer.
—"Song for a Dark Girl"

THE WORLD IS CURIOUS about how religious attitudes, man's most distinctively human disposition, have operated in the formation and in the productivity of its creative people. American curiosity is heightened in the case of Negro authors because religion, through its shape-shifting perseverance under the eyes of slaveholders and their legion descendants South and North, has long held the strands of Negro togetherness. Perhaps the secret of the toughness of those strands, so frequently knotted today as to portend a social revolution, lies partly in the religious affections expressed by Negro writers. For the tie between religion and violence is ancient. America "stubbed its toe," to use a phrase from a poem by Hughes, on the rock that has divided the active Christian conscience from the act of enslaving and dehumanizing the millions for whom it assumed the responsibilities that accompany total arbitrary power. A trail of racial violence and bloodshed under specious Biblical sanction crisscrosses the path of every American and grits the memory of every Negro author, regardless of occasional appearances to the contrary.

The ruts of violence in the wash of a failing Christianity harshly surface some of Hughes's poetry and fiction. His uses of Jesus need to be seen in the perspective of Negro experience and the author's purposes. Extra light gleams over Hughes's fusion of Christ and black people when one sees how his early lapses might have worked with his lifelong attraction to gospel song rituals and fellowship-with-Christ fervor to evolve his concept of an earth-oriented Jesus. In *The Big Sea,* Hughes writes of his hot night, at the age of twelve, on the mourners' bench in Lawrence, Kansas. Some time after he and another boy had been left alone to await the light of Jesus, he heard the boy whisper, "God damn! I'm tired o' sitting here," and saw him rise to be saved. Alone then in a swirl of adjuring songs and prayers, and implored by the sobs of his beloved Auntie Reed, young Hughes finally let the minister lead him to the platform.

Reading Hughes's description of his ordeal later that night, one thinks of the boy Luigi Pirandello, his tears drowned in drums and songs as he marched in the lottery processional to his rich father's house. Like Hughes, the playwright felt his boyhood spiritual integrity thwarted by a sycophantic priest who defrauded him of the good conscience due from his generous attempt to transfer his winning lottery ticket to a poor boy of the church. Hughes records the aftermath of his discovery that prolongation of his "waiting serenely for Jesus" would tilt the ritual askew: "That night, for the last time in my life but one . . . I cried. . . . [my aunt] told my uncle I was crying because . . . I had seen Jesus. But I was really crying because I couldn't bear to tell her that I . . . hadn't seen Jesus, and that now I didn't believe there was a Jesus any more. . . ."

In 1960, Hughes's answer to a question put to him on the radio and television show "Viewpoint" relegated that sad night to its proper place in his development. The question was whether "religious faith of any kind" influenced his work. The author replied: " 'Yes, I would think very much so. I grew up in a not very religious family, but I had a foster aunt who saw that I went to church and Sunday school . . . and I was very much moved, always, by the, shall I say, rhythms of the Negro church, . . . of the spirituals, . . . of those wonderful old-time sermons. . . . And when I began to write poetry, that influence came through. . . .' "[1]

I *Christ on the Road*

Religion in Hughes's poetry is predictably nonsectarian. His faintly satirical cast at the mourners' bench in "Mystery" is far from dogmatic. His stand on one issue, however, could not be more resolute: his opposition to the misuse of religion. In "Sunday Morning Prophecy" (*The New Yorker,* 1942), an old Negro minister, after loudly ending a sin-ripping sermon in a vivid burst of devil's exultation and backsliders' vain cries for deliverance, tersely closes with a "give freely/In the collection basket/That I who am thy shepherd/Might live./Amen!" The poem, typical in its lively actability, is almost insensibly altered by this infusion of straight-faced humor. Incipiently a poem on the misuse of religion by its unduly mercenary agents, the lines lose their faultfinding strength in the old pastor's sudden candor.

An example of a miscarriage of poetic point is Hughes's controversial "Goodbye Christ," a poem which, in the 1930's and 1940's especially, attracted gusts of misinterpretation and calumny. Such repercussions bore upon the refusal of the Los Angeles Civic League in August, 1935, to let Hughes speak in a local YMCA building, and upon the picketing and circularizing by Gerald L. K. Smith's America First Party in April, 1943, at Wayne State University when the Student Council invited the poet to speak there. Hughes's defense of the tough-guy poem as not anti-Christ[2] but as "an ironic protest against racketeering in the churches" and as "anti-misuse of religion" implies that the gist of the poem is in these lines about the New Testament:

> But it's dead now.
> The popes and the preachers've
> Made too much money from it.
> They've sold you [Christ] to too many
> Kings, generals, robbers, and killers—
> Even to the Tzar and the Cossacks. . . .

The fact that the poem also excoriates "big black Saint Becton/ Of the Consecrated Dime," the Harlem preacher shown as a charlatan in *The Big Sea*, has not redeemed features disliked by detractors. Redemption was not needed in the eyes of other readers, such as the Reverend Charles C. Hill, Chairman of the Citizens Committee of Detroit, who answered a letter from Gerald L. K. Smith by saying that Hughes "was expressing the feeling of most Negroes toward white Christianity as displayed every day." Emphasizing that a distortion of Christianity was the poet's point of attack, he added: "I can join Langston Hughes with teeming others in saying 'Goodbye Christ'—the Christ as held up by the white supremacists. . . ."[3]

Turning from this poem, which is the kind of pebble that can always be hurled at some open space in an author's reputation, one might consider two poems related to Hughes's literary humanizing of Jesus. The first, "Judgment Day," in *Selected Poems*, pictures a simple Negro who envisions Jesus as a kind man who speaks as he himself does. It opens thus: "They put ma body in the ground,/Ma soul went flyin' o' the town,/Went flyin' to the stars an' moon/A-shoutin', God, I's comin' soon." The uplifted believer meets a Jesus who comforts him with "don't be 'fraid/Cause you ain't dead."

The more anthropomorphic picture of Jesus in "Ma Lord" (in *The Crisis*, 1927) derives from a quaintly dressed old lady whom the author saw in church when he was a boy in Lawrence. Hughes explained to the moderator of the program "Viewpoint" how her reprimand to the youngsters giggling at her hung in his mind and grew into the poem. The first stanza reads:

> Ma Lord ain't no stuck-up man.
> Ma Lord he ain't proud.
> When he goes a-walkin'
> He gives me his hand
> "You ma friend," he 'lowed.

Hughes went on to say that this poem implies "that when religion places itself at the service of mankind, particularly the humble people, it can . . . strengthen them and guide them. . . ." He added: "There's great beauty in the mysticism of much religious writing, and great help there—but I also think that we live in a world . . . of solid earth and vegetables and a need for jobs . . . and housing. . . ."

Brief as this introduction to his approach to religion is, it gives some personal meaning to the hard task undertaken in "On the Road," the genesis of which story he told in July, 1961, as follows: "I wrote this in Reno, about wandering Negro roustabouts who ran into prejudice in Relief. This was pure fantasy, but also growing out of my actions in Reno . . . and seeing troubled people who were really hungry, and seeing how churches are not equipped to handle a depression." In *I Wonder*, Hughes tells that many penniless Negroes stopped in Reno while hoboing across the nation. They found a hobo jungle, but no Negro section in Reno, then "a very prejudiced town with no public places where Negroes could eat other than two cheap Chinese restaurants."

Written first as "Two on the Road" and revised in Carmel in the fall of 1934,[4] "On the Road" was published by *Esquire* in

January, 1935. Significantly illustrated by a picture of two figures, one more vague than the other, at the far end of a snowy street bearing only one set of footprints, it tells the end-of-the-line adventure of a Negro hobo.

Jumping from a freight train during the depression, Sargeant is too hungry, tired, and sleepy to notice the snow falling on the town. Finding himself on the porch of a parsonage, he is vaguely aware that the minister is shutting the door in his face and directing him brusquely to another relief shelter like the hundreds that have already drawn the color line against him. Moving to the adjoining church, he knocks at the door topped by a stone crucifix and stone Christ. By the time he must break the door open, whites are yelling at him from the street; and two club-swinging policemen have begun to pull and beat him. When Sargeant clings to the church pillars, the crowd helps the officers pull on him; and the church falls into the snow. Rising from the debris, he shoulders the stone pillar, walks away with it, then laughingly throws it six blocks up the street.

In an episode thus removed from reality, Sargeant sees walking beside him the stone Christ, glad to have been broken off the cross. In a friendly, colloquial conversation, Christ says he is bound for Kansas City and recommends the doorless hospitality of the hobo jungle before they separate. At six the next morning, Sargeant tries to jump a freight train's coal car with other hoboes, but finds it full of policemen. One raps his knuckles with a night stick and says, "You ain't out in no jungle now. This ain't no train. You in jail."

These words, a plainer transition between fantasy and reality than the long toss of the pillar, accompany Sargeant's realization that he is in jail for breaking down the church door, that he has been yelling and shaking the bars. Fingers bruised and head bloodied and throbbing, he yells, "I'm gonna break down this door!" Suddenly his thoughts come back to Christ, to end the story: "I wonder if he's gone to Kansas City?"

Hughes told the writer Kay Boyle about this story in 1957:

All I had in mind was cold, hunger, a strange town at night . . . and a black vagabond named Sargeant against white snow, cold people, hard doors, trying to go somewhere, but too tired and hungry to make it—hemmed in on the ground by the same people who hemmed Christ in by rigid rituals surrounding a man-made cross. It developed as a kind of visual picture-story

out of night, snow, man, church, police, cross, doors becoming
bars, then ending with a man shaking the bars, but Christ at least
free on the precarious road—His destination Kansas City, being a
half-way point across the country. . . .[5]

This, and other remarks made at the same time—that the story
was "written completely at one sitting, like a poem," and was
more intriguing to him in word music than in narrative—helps
one to imagine Hughes at work. In the Negro boardinghouse to
which Reno restricted him, after eating his supper of Home Relief
supplies described in *I Wonder,* he sat before his typewriter and
absorbed the mood of a tired, hungry wanderer, a situation not
alien to his experience. Gathering up oppressive, wintry images
to give substance to the racial texture of Reno, he launched his
creating self against the doors he knew were there, responsive all
the while to the music of phrases that came to him.

Because sense is more important than sound, one should first
examine what the story means. Sargeant's odyssey, prolonged by
discrimination and now limited to a search for food and rest before he succumbs to exhaustion, ends at the stone feet of Christ.
At this point the purposes of Sargeant and of mankind join to
enlarge the meaning. Once again Hughes's remarks to Kay
Boyle help:

> I was writing of the little man. . . . I was writing, too, of Jesus
> as a human being whose meaning sometimes has been lost
> through the organization of the church. . . . The function of
> religion in daily life, as the Reverend [Martin Luther] King
> has made it function, is what I was talking about. . . . Sargeant
> had done as much for Jesus in getting Him down off the cross as
> Jesus had done for Sargeant in showing him that even the
> Saviour of men had nowhere to go except to push on. . . .

Before the violence on the steps of the church, involving symbolically all of society, Sargeant's purpose—survival—is blindly
personal. Unlike blind Samson of the Bible, who invokes the aid
of the Lord to pull down the two pillars for his own vengeance,
Sargeant clings to church pillars to preserve himself before the
people—the hostile law and the chain of Philistines—who never
draw his thoughts away from himself.

Only after the church has crumbled and his fellow feeling has
been aroused by another lone traveler does the hobo think of
serving another. The comforting words exchanged by Christ and

the vagabond suggest a triangular religion, connecting one's self, one's fellows, and the Lord. Christ serves the hobo by his example of what might be called "Purity of Predicament," represented here by the ostracism with which society places its mark of infidelity on the brow of those too far removed, by excess either of lowliness or of sublimity, from its dead center. The hobo serves Christ by the destructive though liberating act of flesh mortified by travail. Then, though only in a dream born of pain, he offers the man-made Christ a man's pleasantries, a simple generosity.

This religious positivism agrees with the expressed views of the author. Surely the little man, the first excluded by the selfish rites that immobilize a living Christ, would most benefit from a religion of simple acts of human care. A Christ on the road, crossing half the nation on a single journey, although as humble in spirit and as deprived as a Negro vagabond, could light candles that could never be put out. Sargeant, in freeing Christ though incarcerating himself, unconsciously contributes to the idea of daily brotherhood, of a man-oriented religion.

Although a racial prejudice made more noxious by the depression is broadly reflected in this story, the religious strain is paramount. Systematized religion has failed. Christ is one of the dispossessed, impaled on a cross outside the church. He cannot free himself, yet must come down to the little man, down into the snow to become the companion of a lowly man who cannot enter the church that has petrified the Saviour. Thus the Negro identification with Christ develops. The new comradeship evokes a provocatively new religious image: a Christ who laughs aloud.

The complex style of "On the Road," told in the third person, can only be suggested in this discussion. In this "visual picture-story," a third of the passages characterizing the hobo show his appearance: he is all night, snow, cold, dampness; almost another third depict him bludgeoning or wrestling his way against door-like obstacles. All the images of the story comprise a remarkable pattern of sensations that support the action. The technique, which is like the heaping of sensory words in Hawthorne's "The Minister's Black Veil," can be glimpsed in this partial breakdown of the two hundred and ten patterned images in the six-page story, conveyed in fifty-four repeated words, listed by frequency of use: "door" (28); "snow" (21); "stone" (12); "black" (9); "pull" (8); "cold" (7); "white" (6); "sleepy"

(6); "grab" (6); "fall" (6); "wet" (5); "hungry" (5); "tired" (5); "shut" (5); "push" (5); "cross" (5); "break" (5); "wham" (4); "cell" (4); and "jail" (4). Thus running the scale of images —visual, auditory, tactile, kinesthetic—Hughes mounts a total environment that is repellant, binding, crushing, wintry. Sargeant's world is closing doors, wet snow, cold stone.

Snow as illusion, the sidewalk and church steps as levels of Christianity, and the church edifice as dogma are symbols ably used. The author fuses dream and reality with artistic grace in the hobo's half-conscious montage of cell bars and the iron ladder of a coal car. On the other hand, the author's voice obtrudes unnecessarily at one point, and Christ's language is not perfectly consistent. In this story, included in Bernard Smith's *The Democratic Spirit* (1941) and Lillian Gilkes's *Short Story Craft* (1949), Hughes is master of his material, is poetically alive to every sensory nuance. His identification with Sargeant is complete.

Just as "Ma Lord" and Hughes's comments provide background for "On the Road," other poems and events illuminate "Big Meeting"—the other "Christ story" at the end of *Laughing to Keep from Crying.* "Ballad of Mary's Son" (*The Langston Hughes Reader* [1958]), applying the term "Mary's Boy" to a Negro lynched during Passover, and calling Christ "Mary's Son," merges the persons and deaths so that "This is my body/And this is my blood!" defines a spiritual bond between the crucified Christ and the lynched Negro.

"Christ in Alabama" concerns autobiographical events of a kind never far below the surface of Hughes's mind, events that influence stories like "Big Meeting," "Home" and "Father and Son." The poem caused excitement and threats of violence the night Hughes read it on November 21, 1931, at the University of North Carolina. On a poetry-reading tour of the South financed partly by a grant from the Rosenwald Fund, Hughes had been breathing the air of violence roused by the Scottsboro case in Alabama. And ten days or so earlier, he had felt the tragedy of two deaths caused by the peculiar inhumanity of the South. At Hampton Institute in Virginia, the poet had been approached by Dorothy Maynor, then "a chubby teen-age student choir singer," according to *I Wonder*. The students had selected her to tell him that a Hampton alumnus and new football coach had been beaten to death by an Alabama mob for accidentally parking his car in a "white" parking lot; and that Fisk University's Dean of Women, Juliette Derricotte, whom he had known in Paris and New York, had died the same weekend after an auto wreck in rural Georgia, upon being refused treatment in a nearby "white" hospital.

"Christ in Alabama," written about the Scottsboro Nine, was published with Hughes's satirical article, "Southern Gentlemen, White Prostitutes, Mill-Owners, and Negroes," on the front page of *Contempo*, an unofficial student newspaper at Chapel Hill, the day Hughes arrived. This ironic poem, he states in *I Wonder*, was inspired by the thought of "how Christ, with no human father, would be accepted were He born in the South of a Negro mother." It ends: "Most Holy Bastard/Of the bleeding mouth:/ Nigger Christ/On the cross of the South!" Considering the original title of Hughes's rather sentimental "African Morning" ("Bastard of Gold") and his long, serious interest in the problems of mixed blood, the word "bastard" is as purely genetic as it can be.

And the phrase "Nigger Christ" penetrates beyond devotion to a sympathetic identification molded racially by sharing unmerited suffering and revilement. The literary father of this unfortunate Christ defended his paternity on December 18, 1931, in *The Atlanta World*, a month after its discovery in the South: ". . . anything which makes people think of existing evil conditions is worthwhile. Sometimes in order to attract attention somebody must embody these ideas in sensational forms. I meant my poem to be a protest against the domination of all stronger peoples over weaker ones." This poem induced shock, outrage, and serious thought. Varying proportions of each incited local groups to urge that Hughes be run out of town, hardened the university's resolve to withstand coercion, and enabled the author to shatter the peace further by dining with white students at a white restaurant and, in the words of local Negroes, to "come out, like Daniel, unscathed."

Hughes's attitude toward the climactic events of "Big Meeting" can hardly be understood unless the reader can feel the grain of these events of the author's tour. The source of the narrative itself, he said in September, 1960, was "camp meetings and things I saw as a child." A letter of his specifies one, "held in Pinckney Woods in Lawrence—all Negroes inside the tent, lots of whites gathered outside in cars and otherwise to listen to the music."[6]

"Big Meeting," probably written in October, 1934, in Carmel or Reno,[7] and first published by *Scribner's Magazine* (July, 1935), details a revival in a lantern-lighted tent in the woods. The story is narrated by an unnamed Negro teen-ager who, with his friend Bud, stands under a tree smoking and laughing—somewhat like the whites in autos and buggies, including Mr. Parkes, a drugstore owner who refuses Negroes entry to his store. As the three-part service gets under way with testimonials and songs on this twelfth night of the Big Meeting, whites either variously repeat that they love "to hear darkies singing" or mock Negroes testifying to their troubles. The two teen-agers, amused and embarrassed, watch their own mothers' fervid part in the rocking, clapping, foot-patting, hopping, and handshaking.

The second part of the service begins suddenly as Reverend Duke Braswell strides forward; tall, black, strong, he sings with a voice "roaring like a cyclone." He vividly recounts the death of Christ. Then, with a histrionic style, moaning, gasping, and perspiring with gestic intensity, he grips the congregation with pictures of the crowd at the heels of the cross-bearing Christ, the transfer of the burden to black Simon of Cyrene, and the crucifixion itself. The narrator and Bud are entranced; the congregation moans and weeps. Striding back and forth across the platform, the minister evokes the cursing, spitting, stoning, and name-calling by the mob. "Then," he concludes, stretching his arms high, "they lynched Him on the cross." The narrator hears his mother sing "Were you there when they crucified my Lord?" and sees the nearby whites drive away suddenly and noisily in a cloud of dust. With unexpected tears, at the end, he yells after them: "They're about to call for sinners to come to the mourners' bench. Don't go!"

The boys' ability in this story to humanize their attitude as the suffering underlying the rituals becomes manifest makes the group posture of the whites all the more slack. The boys have exchanged early submission to religious ceremonies for cigarette puffs and street corner jokes, but they retain appreciative memories. The white adults, however, have firmly diked their sympathies inside the color line.

A variety of oblique remarks and phrases contour Southern race relations. During the congregational response to the prayer "guide those in other cities," mothers cry "Help him, Jesus!" as St. Louis, Memphis, and Chicago are named. They remember their faraway children who have fled their homes for a chance at happiness in less racist cities. Part of the pattern is the longing for rest, found only in Jesus, the helplessness amidst injustice and violence: four times the minister emphasizes that Christ's friends could not help him. Racial brutality is expressed as the sweating minister, imitating the sound of crucifying nails, shouts "Bam!" four times, whereupon a woman screams, "Don't drive them nails! For Christ's sake! Oh! Don't drive 'em!" This agony, obviously personal to these Southern Negroes, accentuates the literal and allied meanings of the deep wail of sorrow that has just accompanied the imagined raising of the Saviour to the cross.

The author controls spatially and strategically his theme of Negro identification with Christ. Worked slowly into the first part of the meeting by the unrehearsed expressions of worshipers, it continues unemphasized in the sermon that is divided into three parts that increase in length, importance, and intensity. Reverend Braswell first talks about the power of the lowly, represented by Christ, then about the ability of a man to stand alone, like Jesus, who knew that "all alone by Hisself He would go to His death" and therefore told His weakening friends to "sleep on." The listeners chant "sleep on, sleep on," feeling that each man, for heroic strength, needs only Christ.

Hughes, mindful of the minister's ability, does not voice the main theme when the second part of the sermon turns to images of violence. The minister recalls that Jesus "saw that garden alive with men carryin' lanterns and swords and staves, and the mob was everywhere." Once the word "mob" is used, the author need not even suggest that this congregation has been alerted to special images. The preacher supplies them in abundance, literally filling the tent with key words: "handcuffs," "prisoner," "mob," "chains," "trial," "lies." The reader sees the rituals of violence that these worshipers know too well: the people cry "crucify Him!" because they do not care; soldiers make sport of Jesus, strip Him naked and mock Him laughingly, calling Him "out o' His name." The minister reminds them that "nobody said, 'Stop! That's Jesus!'"—and the congregation adds its own analogy, that the good white Southerner does not face the mob to halt racial brutality in the name of Christianity.

Hughes now lets the minister close the gap between Christ and the Negroes. The preacher's pauses, before the third part, to recapitulate the roles of Peter, Judas, Pilate, and Christ's friends add suspense to his simulated climb, as he bears the heavy cross to Golgotha. "Then a black man named Simon," he continues, "blacker than me [a recurrent phrase in Hughes], come and took the cross"; and he pictures the taunting crowd. The dark minister, making Negro participation on the side of Christ visible by his own stance, and then making it biblical by reference to Simon of Cyrenaica, completes the identification begun before his arrival.

The picture of the crucified Jesus is finished:

> Mob cussin' and hootin' my Jesus! Umn!
> The spit of the mob in His face! Umn!
> . . . .
> They stoned Him first, they stoned Him!
> Called Him everything but a child of God.
> Then they lynched Him on the cross.

Just as "mob" began the Negro verification of Christ's ordeal, the word "lynched" seals the listeners' absorption into the spirit of Christ, given symbolic sanction when the minister stretches his arms upward in the yellow light, his body making "a cross-like shadow on the canvas."

Picturesque scenes direct from life also give sensory zest to this story. The fancies of dreams come down from the testimonial platform, replete with moon-like haloes, silver wings, hoofs of gold. Songs rise humming from ever-moving bodies, swelling as the congregation steeps itself in real sorrows. Sometimes the songs are pulled spontaneously from individual bosoms struck resonantly by a phrase from the platform. Sometimes melody flows from the mass and rolls through the hot tent.

The minister is a man to stare at, "his green-black coat jim-swinging to his knees." Almost like the Reverend Becton scored in "Goodbye Christ," this minister slams the Bible shut and strides to the very edge of the platform before uttering a sermonizing word; but, unlike his wealthy Harlem prototype, he does not plan around the collection plate. His style of chants, half-moans, gasps, and indrawn "umn!" between rapid phrases still lingers, even in some metropolitan pulpits.

Thematically rich within its set limits, "Big Meeting" offers less that is purely literary than does "On the Road." Its view of Negro spirituals and old-time preaching is instructive. The narrative is realistic, the action complete and historically meaningful.

The characters are not full, but they function adequately. The story primarily develops, not individuals, but the profound connection between a single holy martyrdom and a race-wide, centuries-old debasement.

II *The Killers*

In other poems and stories, the viciousness of racial violence, sometimes fatal, is not transformed by religious emphasis but by style. "Southern Mammy Sings" (*Poetry,* May, 1941) begins humorously ("Miss Gardner's in her garden./Miss Yardman's in her yard."), modulates the harshness of its meaning through the use of dialect, then ends:

> Last week they lynched a colored boy.
> They hung him to a tree.
> That colored boy ain't said a thing
> But we all should be free.
>   Yes, m'am!
> We all should be free.
>
> Not meanin' to be sassy
> And not meanin' to be smart—
> But sometimes I think that white folks
> Just ain't got no heart.
>   No, m'am!
> Just ain't got no heart.

These words are a subtle play upon Southern custom and history. The Negro "mammy," mother to Negro youth and motherly nurse to whites who will likely grow up to abuse them, sings (a lovely sign of her contentment) about her travail. Her superficial apology for being so "sassy" as to pass judgment upon the murderous bent of whites accentuates the heroic silence of the boy who died like the victim in Vernon Loggins' story "Neber Said a Mumblin' Word."

It may be surprising that only about a score of the hundreds of poems written by Hughes strongly develop this theme of violence. Yet several of these are memorable. His "Roland Hayes Beaten," imbued with the slow fire of modern Negro spirit, supplied the motto and refrain for the pamphlet printed by the National Association for the Advancement of Colored People (February, 1962), *The Day They Changed Their Minds,* to commemorate the sit-in demonstrations that have brought historic upheaval to the South. The poem is brief:

> Negroes,
> Sweet and docile,
> Meek, humble, and kind:
> Beware the day
> They change their minds!
>
> Wind
> In the cotton fields,
> Gentle breeze:
> Beware the hour
> It uproots trees!

The Negro Handbook for 1944 reads: "July 11 [1942]—Roland Hayes, internationally famous tenor, was beaten by three white policemen in Rome, Ga., where he lived with his family, following a brief argument that his wife had with a shoe store clerk." In the poem, Hughes elevates the gentle artist's ordeal into a tense warning. The repetition of *beware*, the contrast between *day* and *hour*, the analogy of the wind that brings both static sweetness and rushing holocaust—all are restrained prophecy. The physically precarious balance in the single-word lines carries much of the meaning. The poet's steadying irony insured artistic quality.

1. *"Home"*

Emotionally close to this poem is "Home," the first story written after Hughes's return from Yokohama. Composed in San Francisco in September, 1933, it appeared the following May in *Esquire* as "The Folks at Home," illustrated in color.[8] The narrative develops, said the author, various stories told by Negro performers back from Europe. He added, in July, 1961: "Louis Jones was studying and playing in Europe when I was over there. He achieved some concert note. I had in mind someone like him who might have come from a town in the Deep South. Roy is a real person in a sense."

The story opens with Hughes's narration of the return home to Hopkinsville, Missouri, of ailing Roy Williams, a violinist who has toured the world for several years. Weakened by a tubercular cough, he has made a sentimental journey home to die. Following a two-page flashback relating his pained closeness to poverty abroad, in Section II Roy moves through the racial insults of white loafers at the station. Section III contains a lyrical burst celebrating a Missouri summer, then pursues the contrast with Section II through a one-page flow of loving welcome, praise, and news from Roy's mother. An equally brief Section IV describes the colorful, perfumed filling up of the church where Roy is to give a home-coming concert. Section V opens with three pages of sustained lyricism in which Roy, standing fevered on the rostrum, muses nostalgically over his mother's sacrifices for his musical career. As it ends, he is praised by a cheaply dressed white woman, Miss Reese, who, his mother tells him, is "an old maid musicianer at the white high school."

In the final and longest section, the wasting artist plays for Miss Reese's sprawling students, who later tell their parents that "a dressed-up nigger had come to the school with a violin and played a lot of funny pieces," that the teacher had "grinned all over herself" and even bowed. One night Roy, hollow-cheeked and trembling, walks the street in spats and yellow gloves. Imagining Tauber singing, he does not hear the villagers cursing him; but he recognizes Miss Reese when she bows and speaks. He removes his hat and gloves and extends his hand. She screams when a fist strikes Roy's head, thus activating the hatred in a crowd emerging from a movie. Imaginations leap to the image of rape; they trample and pummel Roy and spit in his face. The screaming whites kick and drag him through town to the woods.

The final paragraph was unforgettable to book reviewers: "The little Negro . . . began to choke on the blood in his mouth. And the roar of their voices and the scuff of their feet were split by the moonlight into a thousand notes like a Beethoven sonata. And when the white folks left his brown body, stark naked, strung from a tree . . . it hung there all night, like a violin for the wind to play."

All violence can be misleading. It means little in itself, just as a striking fist means little in isolation from the mind directing it and the circumstances so narrowly stimulating that mind. Even the title "Home" gives texture to the brutality that is rather foreign to the basically sentimental main action. The reader must temporarily turn away from the savagery in order that other themes may fill the contours made for them. Roy, traveling in slowly disintegrating Europe, embodies the role of art in life. A sympathetic, humane man, he is the touchstone of sane good taste and decency by which one knows that Europe is in decay. He carries beauty, in the form of his music and his sensibilities, into the heart of adamant unconcern for the poor and helpless. He is grieved that young beauty must be debased by prostitution. Playing in happy cabarets, he images the destitute children slumped in doorways he must pass. Roy is man's wish for beauty and charity, crushed when European jackboots are fitted, or when home-town hatred is loosed.

Art, creating beauty, can thrive only when conditions approximate those of home—not the grossness Roy finds abroad where eaters of caviar take no thought of searchers for crumbs, but the care in his mother's greeting: "Son, I'm glad you's done come home. What can Ma cook for you?" Her several references to foods are more than realistic detail. Carefully contrasted with Europe's hunger and immorality, they are part of the home-like love that fosters art and beauty. Totally ignorant of classical music, Roy's mother can only vaguely express the bond between beauty and goodness: "Honey, when you plays that violin o' your'n it makes me right weak, it's so purty. . . . God's done give you a gift!"

The artist, finding the world "rotten," attempts the impossible: a return to the same home he left. Not only his cough is killing him; it is the *Zeitgeist* abroad, a spiritual decay inimical to his nature and to his beauty. His physical wasting at home is medically explainable, but it also accords with the malignant spirit he finds there: the native counterpart of Europe's hunger. What he yearns for, escape from decadence, not from death itself, is the fresh substance of the author's lyrical exuberance before Roy meets his mother: "Sing a song of Dixie, cotton bursting in the sun, shade of chinaberry trees, persimmons after frost has fallen. Hounds treeing possums October nights. O, sweet potatoes, hot, with butter in their yellow hearts."

The melding of life and art—seen in "The Blues I'm Playing," written the same month—occurs naturally in the fragmented thoughts of sick Roy, playing Massenet in the church (ellipses are Hughes's):

This is the broken heart of a dream come true not true. This is music, and me, sitting on the doorstep of the world needing you. . . . O, body of life and love with black hands and brown limbs and white breasts and a golden face with lips like a violin

bowed for singing. . . . Steady, Roy! It's hot. . . . This, the dream
and the dreamer, wandering in the desert from Hopkinsville to
Vienna in love with a streetwalker named Music. . . . Listen, you
bitch, I want you to be beautiful as the moon in the night on the
edge of the Missouri hills. I'll make you beautiful. . . .

This passage invites study never necessary for scenes of violence
like those that end the story. Roy's diction itself, combining the
colloquial with the formal in its description of art, merges two
forms of experience, just as "wandering in the desert" links
Missouri with Vienna, stretching the body of art in a synthesis
of man's achievements. The "dream come true not true" joins the
deeds of a musician who lived to be seventy, Massenet, with the
abortive dreams of a violinist who died young and who needed
art to help him briefly survive a poisonous environment. The
subsequent impassioned salute to an art that gratefully employs
rather than abuses racial differences is the heart of the passage.
The final lines, showing the earthiness of Roy's love for his
music, also reveal the ego that drives an artist to transcend the
vulgar body of life in his reach for its spirit.

The motif of Southern racial habits almost coarsens the texture
of the story, if one begins with esthetic considerations. The
action, however, is grounded in those customs. Hughes merely
alludes to some, like economic and educational discrimination;
but he pointedly shows white resentment of good attire for
Negroes. His most significant reflections of this kind are somewhat subtle. At the church concert, for example, Roy, instead of
taking professional pleasure in Miss Reese's attention, wonders
suspiciously, "What do you want from me?" Undergoing the
perversions of racial prejudice, he distrusts the woman because
of her color—in contrast to his gratitude to a Parisian girl who
helped him regain his strength. Later, trampled and bleeding, he
wonders why Miss Reese spoke to him on the street. The
savagery of her townsmen has become the identifying mark of
her race; she is no longer a music lover but just another treacher-
ous white woman. The likelihood that Roy has been spat upon
by a childhood playmate completes the wretched turnabout.

Commentary on racial violence as a psychological oddity—and
on the author as a social observer—is implicit in the final scenes.
The sincerity of Miss Reese is a bitter irony: her scream, caused
by genuine fright, fatally ignites the ritual of group homicide.
Hughes, by selecting young "ruffians" to be the killers, exempts

the ordinarily humane citizens from material blame and suggests that the emotionalism and delusion that arouse brutality are typical only of the immature minority. The extent and nature of the blame deserved by other citizens, although morally important, are not made relevant to the action.

Hughes makes sure use of his repetitions. Carrying contrasts and interacting ironies, they usually hold to an axis between Missouri and Europe, between ugliness and beauty: the station loafers versus Roy's mother, Roy's sensitivity versus the barbarity of his attackers. Reflecting a similar pattern, Roy's mother believes her son honored by a request to play at the white school; she is unaware that a Carnegie Hall or a Salle Gaveau would be much more fitting.

The figurative language is usually vivid: "the glittering curtains of Roy's jazz were lined with death." Some images are sharply effective: girls in church are "powdered bonbon faces . . . with red mouths pointed at Roy." Other techniques are questionable: the uninterrupted length of some dialogue, the usefulness in the plot of Roy's brothers and sister, the faltering point of view in Roy's soliloquy.

Realistic fiction exposing American racism has often been repressed, and "Home" provides an example. Speaking at the National Assembly of Authors and Dramatists Symposium on "The Writer's Position in America," at New York's Alvin Theatre on May 7, 1957, Hughes stated, without mentioning the name of the story, "Home": "I once sent one of my best known short stories . . . to one of our oldest and foremost American magazines. The story was about racial violence in the South. It came back to me with a very brief little note saying the editor did not believe his readers wished to read about such things."[9] The editors of *Atlantic Monthly* wrote his agent on January 8, 1934: "Why is it that authors think it is their function to lay the flesh bare and rub salt in the wound? ["Home"] is both powerful and delicate, but we cannot forget that most people read for pleasure, and certainly there is no pleasure to be found here."[10]

"Home" does have a power whose delicacy throws it into vivid relief. Sometimes the style has the softness of Roy's yellow gloves or of his autumn reminiscences of Parisian evenings; sometimes it has the hardness of a swift blow to the head. Both music and discord are combined to reveal two civilizations. The passages of violence are extreme in meaning rather than in style, the extremity of unwelcome truth rather than of ungrounded exaggeration. A piece of art, this story discloses Hughes's ability to transform revolting fact into tough beauty.

2. *"Father and Son": the Poems and the Story*

Racial brutality as a theme for an American writer explains itself, especially when the writer is a Negro. Mention has been made of violence that came early, both directly and vicariously, into Hughes's life, including instances in Mexico, Chicago, Virginia, and Alabama. One of his earliest poems showing deep response to racial violence, "The South," first published in *The Crisis* (June, 1922), begins:

> The lazy, laughing South
> With blood on its mouth.
> The sunny-faced South,
>   Beast-strong,
>   Idiot-brained.
> The child-minded South
> Scratching in the dead fire's ashes
> For a Negro's bones.

The poet continues by picturing the South as "Seductive as a dark-eyed whore," cruel, "Honey-lipped, syphilitic." The most extensive meaning is captured in two lines: "And I, who am black, would love her/But she spits in my face." This poem, written when Hughes was barely out of his teens, ably employs the effects natural to the unpredictable movements half-anticipated in an adult idiot happened upon after the climax of some brutal deed. The quoted lines further reflect some somber dementia oddly mixed with confused self-pity. The stresses of juvenile, irrational passion that supply energy to the unmoving images are played against such unrevealing words as *sunnyfaced* and *magnolia-scented*. The lines are vigorous, economically sharp (except for lines 9-11, unquoted), and they mix some biblical rhythm with short verses that seem to halt and tersely revise complimentary phrases. The South, seen by a Negro trapped in its dangers and desires, is painted with tense, brusque strokes in Hughes's earliest period.

"Song for a Dark Girl" (*The Crisis*, May, 1927) employs a specific instance of violence. The first two stanzas read:

Way Down South in Dixie
(Break the heart of me)
They hung my black young lover
To a cross roads tree.

Way Down South in Dixie
(Bruised body high in air)
I asked the white Lord Jesus
What was the use of prayer.

The violence in this poem is subordinated to grief. The violence is an assumption, a strong one, based on the steady history of lynchings (averaging fifty a year in the early 1920's), the place of the killing, and the condition of the corpse. The conventionally pleasant South, ironically pictured in the nostalgic refrain borrowed from a thumping Dixieland tune, is juxtaposed with the heartbreak of a tortured girl. The severely simple technique, using only six different words longer than one syllable, matches the drained hopelessness. The separation of consciousness and bereaved flesh, made more anguished by the poet's "the heart of me" rather than "my heart," is of a piece with the girl's shriveled religious faith: she knows that Christianity is often the racial instrument of whites. This well-written poem, ending with a sterile concentration of feeling ("Love is a naked shadow/ On a gnarled and naked tree"), shows Hughes's early ability to individualize images and events highly symbolic to Negroes without lessening social meaning.

Similar emphases are found in lesser poems like "Blue Bayou," "Silhouette," "Flight," and "Lynching Song," all concerned with lynchings. Racially motivated police brutality, North and South, is the subject of "Third Degree," "Who But the Lord?," and "The Ballad of Margie Polite." Connected also with racial customs, but only obliquely related to violence, are "Cross" and "Mulatto," inseparable from the final story to be treated in this chapter, "Father and Son."

These two poems and the story are representative of a substantial theme in Hughes's works: the problems of Negroes of mixed parentage.[11] In the chapter "Poetry" in *The Big Sea*, Hughes writes that his interest in such problems began in Lawrence, where he played with a blond boy "whose mother was colored and whose father, the old folks whispered, was white," a boy who later passed for white himself.

In *I Wonder* (in "Making Poetry Pay"), Hughes calls the poem "Cross" (*The Crisis,* December, 1925) his "ace in the hole" at poetry readings. His description of his reading technique—which reveals his custom of dispensing facts of Negro history from the lecture platform—has interest:

> The first line—intended to awaken all sleepers—I would read in in a loud voice:
>> My old man's a white old man. . . .
>
> And this would usually arouse any who dozed. Then I would pause before continuing in a more subdued tone:
>> My old mother's black.
>
> Then in a low, sad, thoughtful tragic vein:
>> But if ever I cursed my white old man
>> I take my curses back.

Hughes's poem then revokes possible maternal curses, and it ends:

> My old man died in a fine big house,
> My ma died in a shack.
> I wonder where I'm gonna die,
> Being neither white nor black.

The poet's description closes thus: "Here I would let my voice trail off into a lonely silence. Then I would stand quite still for a long time, because I knew I had the complete attention of my listeners again."

This poem written in 1925 and the author's testimony regarding its sure-fire effectiveness on the rostrum mark an important fact about Hughes's contemporary audience. Although "Cross" is a mediocre poem to the analytical-critical reader, it apparently serves many listeners as a complete, affecting experience because the protagonist's moral character is only vaguely, even ambiguously, related to his situation. The logic of the concluding two lines is poor, just as the protagonist's cursing of his "black old mother" weakens sympathy for him. Yet Hughes, in his unfailing platform delivery, has proved the emotional power in the lines. It is likely that "Cross," after its first two lines, loses its identity as a poem and becomes a dynamic creation in the imagination of an American audience caught up in its resentments and fears. The very unresolved nature of the topic of miscegenation in America, irrational as it is, makes the end of the poem emotionally acceptable. The allusions to slavery and modern economic discrimination (the big house versus the shack), the expression of Negro pride (the cursing of the white man), and subtler indications of white dereliction—all leaving the moral initiative in the hands of a Negro—place the poem in the spiritual mainstream of modern Negro thought.

The other poem, "Mulatto," related to Hughes's 1935 drama, is generally not emphasized by Hughes in the sequence of works leading to "Father and Son" and *The Barrier*. Yet "Mulatto" is more strictly faithful to the spirit of the story and the opera than "Cross" is. In the passage in *The Big Sea* preceding Hughes's recollection of the mulatto child in Lawrence, he writes of the former poem:

> In New York in the summer of 1926, I wrote . . . "Mulatto" which was published in the *Saturday Review of Literature*. I worked harder on that poem than on any other. . . . Almost every night that summer I would . . . change it. When I read it one night at a gathering at James Weldon Johnson's, Clarence Darrow said it was more moving than any other poem of mine he had read.

"Mulatto" opens as follows:

> *I am your son, white man!*
>
> Georgia dusk
> And the turpentine woods.
> One of the pillars of the temple fell.
>
> > *You are my son!*
> > *Like hell!*
>
> The moon over the turpentine woods.
> The Southern night
> Full of stars,
> Great big yellow stars.
> > What's a body but a toy?
> > Juicy bodies
> > Of nigger wenches
> > Blue black
> > Against black fences.
> > O, you little bastard boy,
> > What's a body but a toy?

This dramatic dialogue offers a tensely individualized conflict between father and son that is hardened by the vigor and scorn of the words and broadened by carefully placed, suggestive details from nature. The son's adamant voice opens the poem, but is transformed into a passive Negro feminine presence exuberantly recalled by the white father, who feels half-pleasurably nagged in his fancied return to the conception and infancy of his son. The poet, employing the past awakened in the white man, leaves him musing and moves the growing child swiftly through years of hostile rejection by his white half-brothers—implying virtual estrangement from his father, whom he no longer reminds of sexual freedom in the Negro quarter. *"Niggers ain't my brother"* is the rebuff so ungrammatically worded as to show the displacement of reason and truth by blind social restrictions. In the last third of the poem, the father's reminiscences of woods, stars, and exploitable black women are slightly rephrased, indistinctly merging the author's voice with the father's. At the end, *"I am your son, white man!"* is repeated as a challenging accusation, weaker now, yet taking precedence over the phrases enclosing it, the author-father's echoes of earlier sensuous memories. Oddly, this is the father's poem. The delicious memories, the unweakened sense of arbitrary power to take and to withhold, the expansive portents of nature, even though ironically misconstrued—all are his. The son is the catalyst, but the father glows. The author expands his profoundly racial material and so convincingly explores a white father's subconscious that the poet's own hovering irony becomes inseparable from the ambivalent remembrances of his subject.[12]

"Father and Son," thematically germinal, then, in other works, can hardly be traced to a time and place. Written in November, 1933, in Carmel,[13] the story closed *The Ways of White Folks.* The author remarked in September, 1960, that it came "from many common miscegenation stories. This was a build-up," he added, "of stories I have heard all my life." Almost twice as long as "Poor Little Black Fellow" but nearest it in length, "Father and Son" opens in the spring of 1931 at Colonel Thomas Norwood's Big House Plantation in Georgia. The Colonel, in his sixties, awaits with feigned casualness the homecoming of twenty-year-old Bert, his youngest son by his Negro mistress, Coralee Lewis, who has kept his house for thirty years and borne his five children. He recalls that Bert is like him: handsome, bright, bad, and now scholastic leader and football captain at the colored institute. Section I ends as the Colonel, surrounded by Negroes, speaks to Bert; but, sensing a "stiffness like steel nearing steel," the father ignores his son's extended hand.

Sections II and III are a flashback in Cora's memory. She recalls how the Colonel teased her as a boy, how his later affections were sealed one night by an oak tree in a conquest reminiscent of "Mulatto," and how he moved her into the Big House after delicate Mrs. Norwood died. Section IV, containing two additional, smoothly introduced flashbacks, begins with one about Bert's ride home in a Ford with his oldest brother Willie, who calls his boldness "crazy." Bert's recollections reveal background: Cora's children had to live apart from her in a shack, but she influenced the Colonel to give them extra education. Young Sally is intelligent but bound to Georgia, and Bertha has clung to Chicago after one trip there. Bert also wants to live in the North, but knows his mother wants him to spend this last summer with her.

Section V lyrically salutes the transforming power of Bert's imported creed ("Let old knotty-headed Willie go on being a white-folk's nigger if he wants to, I won't!"), then returns to the handshaking scene. Sections VI and VII raise the tension by Bert's refusal to do field labor, by a nearly fatal beating the foreman Talbot gives a Negro, and by news of the Scottsboro trials. Bert inflames Junction whites on the final day of the story by demanding equal consideration in stores and by fighting off three men who assault him in the post office after he objects to receiving insufficient change.

In Section VIII, the furious Colonel commands Bert to "talk like a nigger should to a white man," excoriates him racially while holding a pistol, and orders him out of the county. Bert, with "the steel of the gun . . . between them," finally strangles his father. Told by his grief-stricken mother to run for the swamp, he takes the gun and leaves by the front door, that has always been forbidden him. The rest of Section VIII consists primarily of four scenes of harsh interrogation and violence on the part of whites, interspersed with four scenes of temporary derangement on the part of Cora. She urgently handles and addresses the body of the Colonel, berating the corpse alternately for not rising to help Bert and for joining the mob's pursuit of him. Amidst screams and bullets, Bert returns shooting and goes upstairs, one bullet left. Cora delays the mob until the shot is fired upstairs.

Section IX, the concluding page, opens the next morning, revealing "a bloody and unrecognizable body hanging in the public square at the Junction." Some onlookers, knowing Bert was taken dead, are unappeased. The story ends with this head-lined article from an evening paper: "A large mob late this after-noon wrecked [*sic*] vengeance on the second of two Negro field hands, the murderers of Colonel Thomas Norwood. . . . Bert Lewis was lynched last night, and his brother, Willie Lewis, to-day. The sheriff of the county is unable to identify any members of the mob. . . . The dead man left no heirs."

This third-person story, stemming partly from Hughes's "poetic tragedy," forbidden to Philadelphians and almost banned in Chicago, has violent scenes that, again, might obscure the artistry. Certainly Hughes wants to show that racial violence is a way of life in the Deep South, perpetrated by low-class whites but openly sanctioned or actively tolerated by upper classes. Colonel Norwood was a member of a recent lynch mob. The story often mentions the brutal beating he gave his son for calling him "papa" in front of whites. Cora's response to that ("I ain't bearin' him children for to beat 'em to death") defines an undercurrent of her emotional life. It joins her foreboding many years later as she brings Bert to his father for the fatal talk: "Son, you be careful. I didn't bear you for no white man to kill." The new term "white man" shows her long-borne realization of the barrier between father and son, between father and mother —one capable of swiftly destroying filial and domestic bonds.

Cora, not the author this time, blames the lower classes for most of the violence. To her, Bert is "runnin' from po' white trash what ain't worth de little finger o' nobody's got [Norwood] blood in 'em." The ritual of psychopathic attack signalled by a woman's scream, carried out in the post office, is ended by the lynching of servile Willie. Hughes, asked in July, 1961, whether he had any moral in mind when adding the lynching, replied: "Just to show how bad they could be; they go from bad to worse once they get on that savage rampage. Also to show there's no being a 'good nigger' in the South. They'll kill them too, if they feel like it."

Two passages near the end of the story picture the unequal forces at work in a racist environment. Bert, headed upstairs with his single bullet, looks back at "this little brown woman standing there waiting for the mob," which breaks inside but stops before her before running on. Cora stands "looking down at them silently," unmoving. The diminutiveness and courage of Cora, the rush and cessation of movement, the pitting of mass against individual, and the superior physical placement of Cora (like that of Sargeant on the church steps) all have sure meaning in the context of racial deployment of forces in the South. The official lies and omissions in the newspaper further align on the Negro side the moral power which alone prevails over deep abuse.

Two other themes largely concern the actions of whites: interracial amours and Negro education. The liaison between the Colonel and Cora, the story goes, "like that of so many between Negro women and white men in the South, began without love." (Hughes's program note for *The Barrier*, mailed to the American Theatre Society in 1950, calls that related opera "a tragedy of love.")[14] Instead of exploiting this love—as Broadway producer Martin Jones was to do in 1935—Hughes strongly infuses Cora's romantic memories with references to overriding economic motives for Negro participation in such love affairs. Aunt Tobie Lewis, finding her daughter Cora pregnant, advises: "It's better'n slavin' in the cotton fields. I's known colored women what's worn silk dresses and lived like queens on plantations right here in Georgy." As for white management of Negro education, the author is directly critical. Bert's college, he qualifies, is "what they call a college in Negro terms in Georgia," and county educational policy is "to let Negroes remain unlettered" so that they will make better laborers.

Other motifs concern activities and attitudes of Negroes. Colonel Norwood orders an unsuccessful Baptist revival: "a useful outlet for sullen overworked darkies." Old Sam, a house servant, fearing rightly that he might end his days in a bonfire, cries out, "Lawd, is I sinned?"—and gives the lawless white mob the office of religious retribution. Besides these glances at religion, one sees intraracial color bias in light-skinned Bert's unopposed, sometimes scandalous, merrymaking in Atlanta society. Allusions to Negro emphases in the concept of death as rest recall the motif of weariness in "One Christmas Eve" and "Big Meeting."

The strongest theme hardly concerns race. Although race

heightens the clash between father and son, the crucial issues (a son's feeling about his home and about his father's recognition of his whole being) could be just as formidable if color were replaced by another complication. The conflict is reflected in Hughes's techniques of characterization. The following breakdown reveals expanded meaning behind the two portraits. The numbers represent round percentages of the totals of characterizing phrases or passages (fifty-nine for Bert, and forty-nine for his father) devoted to various means of portraiture:

Bert		Colonel Norwood	
Attitude:	44	Attitude:	43
Action:	17	Action:	20
Appearance:	14	Appearance:	2
Environment:	12	Environment:	10
Emotional reaction:	7	Emotional reaction	16
Effect on others:	5	Effect on others:	6
Words:	2	Words:	2

The remarkably close correlation between the frequencies of use of attitude to compare father and son shows the equal soundness with which Hughes conceives the two characters in terms of the general trait that most naturally and thoroughly searched out their mutual tragedy. The sharp differences in the use of appearance and emotional reaction confirm the importance to Bert of his looks, which bewildered him as a boy and emboldened him as a young man. The more than double attention given the Colonel's emotions, coupled with their nature, shows his disturbances to be not only personal and true to his temper, but broadly societal and expressing the resentment of the white townspeople.

The portrait of the Colonel appears more complete than that of Bert because his title raises an abundance of long-used details and because Hughes adds such humanizing touches. Within the rigid limitations of his society, which finally inflate his most intemperate and animal qualities, he is generous, faithful, and strong. He is enough of a father to feel pride and pain because of his son. He is enough of a husband to feel "something very like love," says the author, for the woman who has "supervised his life" and borne his children. His anguish derives from his race and region, as does his ultimate callousness.

Bert is new to the experience and imagination of many readers: he is a hotheaded, proud Southerner—who happens to be colored. He comes to life through the rather narrow compass of his resentment, boldness, and pride—all concentrated in his attitude toward his father. For Bert is more son than Negro. Some readers who empathize with him as a frustrated son may not believe in him as a flesh-and-blood Negro, for want of more racially identifying marks. The author supports Bert's reality through the boy's weaknesses, not through the pedestrian use of clichés.

Bert is central in the symbolic approach to the story. The dust clouds in which he arrives and later careens in the Ford past his cane-waving father portend the catastrophic nature of his presence and his creed, "not to be a *white folks' nigger.*" Whatever the phrase itself does not achieve, the author supplies at once with winged lyricism: "Bow down and pray in fear and trembling, go way back in the dark afraid; or work harder . . . or stumble and learn; or raise up your fist and strike—but once the idea comes . . . you'll never be the same again. Oh, test tube of life! Crucible of the South, find the right powder and . . . the cotton will blaze and the cabins will burn and the chains will be broken and men, all of a sudden, will shake hands, black men and white men, like steel meeting steel!" Bert is symbolic of the author's insistent hope: of his vision of some cataclysmic, healing change in the nation's body and spirit.

Other symbols and images are effective. Negro voices and laughter and the front porch are symbols employed to add tension, suspense, and historical meaning. Images perform an unusual function, moving from the ripple of brown backs in green cotton, through beguiling tableaux of Cora playing in the dust as a child, to the sunset as a "river of blood" and the lights of honking autos beaming through the woods. This painful change in imagery, Hughes suggests, as it shifts from nostalgia and innocent charm to animal brutality, is made imperative by the anomaly of Southern attitudes. Linking the beauty and ugliness of life, mainly limiting the former to the few years of youth, the contrast is faithful both to the essential condition of man and to modern racial variations of it.

Other techniques deserve analysis, among them the juxtaposition of the cruel and the tender—not consciously planned, the author said when asked about it in July, 1961. But the most skillful and subtle effect of all is produced when Hughes envelops and infuses Cora's "mad scenes" (which are mixed with and terminated by mob scenes—a total of eleven pages) with remarkable images of flight. Thirty-five are running footfalls, and three of the remaining four are vivid sense impressions.

These images of flight are ably patterned. Ten are concentrated in the two pages preceding the longest mad scene. Half are urgent terms (like "Run, chile!") that set in motion Bert's flight through the trees. The other half are images of running white men, a hurtling auto getting into high gear, the blood-like rush of sunset streaming after Bert. Ten of the next group of fourteen show Bert running; four, the Colonel. In the next group of seven, Sam and the cook Livonia join the flight, and the sound of "feet running, running, running" spreads through the woods. The last seven skillfully halt the running. The fugitive's feet seem still in motion when, back at the house, he tells his mother he has been fleeing seemingly "for hours." In a slowdown of motion after the mob breaks in, the running images reverse; and a leader of the unsteady mob almost induces stillness by saying, "Keep still, men. He's armed." Then comes the perfectly timed device that cuts off resurgent movement: the shot upstairs. Artfully, Cora's stepping aside intensifies the cessation. Thus Hughes gives almost a fourth of his story—the clusters of images having sustained their effect throughout intervening passages—a background of tension and excited motion, properly collapsed before the degradation of the final morning.

Although Hughes makes errors (the "hissing" of some non-sibilant words and the assignment of the same name, Jim, to the storekeeper and one undertaker), the story is admirably written. It is replete with individual and racial meaning, for the author as well as for the reader. It has no songs, no glee, no real romance. That befits the tragic story of a son who cannot be a son, of a father whose mortal debt to his own race is payable in that son's pride and blood. Father and son, white and black, in this story become forces that, in Hughes's own metaphor, are steel approaching steel. The author provides the collision; and the reader, left with the enormity of patricide and the bestiality of useless killing, must conclude why this grim reckoning had to be.

These poems and stories reveal the author's comprehension of Negro folk culture, his awareness of historical and individual forces at work in Southern life, and his implicit vision of a decisive moral encounter that will bring brotherhood to America. In his poems on racial exploitation and brutality, he reveals abomination as well as sensitivity to human weakness and valor. In his poems on religion, he shows the road not taken by the Negro folk in the wake of faltering Christianity (for "Goodbye Christ" and "Christ in Alabama" can be so understood); and he preserves authentic cameos of old-style Negro believers, bound to common people the world over by the simplicity and durability of their faith. From his related short stories, which powerfully condense and transform the central anguish of a whole race, one might say, remembering Yeats's contemplation of seemingly needless death, that "a terrible beauty is born."

CHAPTER 5

Love, Life, and Negro Soul

Three hundred years in the deepest South,
But God put a song and a prayer in my mouth.
God put a dream like steel in my soul.
  —"The Negro Mother"

IN HIS LIFELONG EXPLORATION of the Negro condition and the Negro soul, Hughes has remained alert to his total environment. His portraits of his own people usually appear on a canvas large enough to accommodate some vital part of American national life. Any subject suggested by an intimate word like *love,* or by a cosmic word like *life,* seems to expand. The expansion is genuine and natural in Hughes's topics, illuminated uniquely by racial insights and national attitudes. Interracial love thus appears inevitable as a theme in the works of any writer immersed in the real lives of Negroes, termed "the American untouchables" by Kingsley Davis of Columbia University.[1]

Ambivalence toward the Negroes who were a joyous fad in the 1920's is shown in their countrymen's antipathy toward them that is still institutionalized in various states by laws forbidding intermarriage, placement of white children in interracial homes, and similar personal alliances. Such restrictions mean that love across the color line is a subject vital to most Americans, keenly perturbing to many. Poems and stories concerning the topic, their literary value aside, invite attention.

I *Love Across the Color Line*

Just as interracial love scarcely concerns most Negroes, it gets little attention in Hughes's works. Of the five poems that develop the theme, two were discussed in Chapter III, "Red Silk Stockings" and "Ruby Brown." The other three are limited in compass, but each makes its point through some fact reminiscent of the 1920's. "Mellow," in *Montage,* is an ironic snap of unemotional detachment; it records the thrill, partly vengeful and partly reckless, when "Into the laps/of black celebrities/ white girls fall." "Harlem Night Club," in *Africa Sings* (1929), is a single-glance tableau of interracial flirtation against a background of heady jazz. "The New Cabaret Girl," in *Fine Clothes*, is a brusquely sympathetic portrait of the so-called tragic mulatto, this one a "little yaller gal/Wid blue-green eyes" who could not leave her troubles at home. Hughes's poetic treatment of the theme is relatively slight and is confined to his earliest poems.

Four stories provide a more revealing index of the author's responses to the subject. "A Good Job Gone," "Little Dog," "Red-Headed Baby," and "Mother and Child" differ in seriousness and in style. Hughes, speaking in September, 1960, of "A Good Job Gone," said: "I knew several New York stories like this." He added the next July: "There were several quite beautiful and well-kept women in the Renascence period. I didn't know of anyone who went crazy." This story, the third written in the New Moscow Hotel and composed March, 1933,[2] first appeared in *Esquire* (April, 1934).

It is narrated by the houseboy of Mr. Lloyd, a zealous New York philanderer who falls in love with a golden-brown chorus girl from Harlem named Pauline. After a physically degrading quarrel with her over her dark Harlem lover, Mr. Lloyd is forced to resume his bouts with white women. His nights become maudlin with drunken memories of Pauline. His derangement is finally betrayed when he makes amorous advances upon the door and women's photographs, and he is placed in a padded cell, thinking himself both stud horse and lion.

Esquire, before publication, sounded out public receptiveness to the story. The *San Francisco Spokesman* of January 25 said in part: "Previously, stories which told the truth about miscegenation . . . were banned. They were all right as long as the white hero repented . . . and returned to his own color. But going to the devil for the love of a mulatto—NEVER! Thanks to Langston Hughes, the truth is out. . . ." These lines, which reflect a second racial publishing policy, that restricting treatment of Indians to the kind of clichés found in Beadle's Pocket Novels, echo all but two of the nearly twenty *Esquire* readers' letters in the February issue. Into "The Sound and Fury" column of *Esquire,* readers poured their feelings from May to September. Especially vituperative was the exchange between John Grimball Wilkins of

Charleston, South Carolina, and D. Roland Mapes of New York City. Wilkins termed Mapes an "off-shade Yankee," who in trying "to insult a Southerner . . . is like the old possum dog out in the cypress swamp . . . following a dangerous trail." When Wilkins offered to come to New York and "settle the matter on the spot," his opponent revealed his own address (which *Esquire* refused to do) and invited him to "cake walk up here with his hound dogs."

"A Good Job Gone" is hardly subtle; the love is as plain as the "hugging and kissing" described. Inevitability modifies the sexual lure of Harlem to which Mr. Lloyd succumbs, for he has made it his business to canvass all feminine types. With mythical ease, Pauline displaces her predecessors, becoming another Luani of the Jungles as her white lover deteriorates in his lunatic failure to survive her departure. The promiscuousness of Mr. Lloyd and the economic motivation of Pauline indicate that the author intends no delicacy of emotion. Hughes primarily examines the rich white philanderer as a type, not even telling what this particular roué looks like. One must guess his age from the length of his marriage. His attitudes and desires motivate almost all the action; but colorful scenes, moreso than analytic exposition, reveal his thinking.

Pauline, the "sugar-brown" who has Mr. Lloyd "standing on his ears," has the sparkle of the flapper and the speakeasy. She is also just a friendly colored girl who, like Claudina of "Poor Little Black Fellow," prefers her own race. "Call me Pauline," she tells the houseboy; "I ain't white." Her faint scorn erupts into the blast she delivers over the unconscious form of Mr. Lloyd, felled by her whiskey bottle: " 'A white bastard!' she said. 'Just because they pay you, they always think they own you. . . . I laugh with 'em and they think I like 'em. Hell, I'm from Arkansas where the crackers lynch niggers in the streets. How could *I* like 'em?' " Her bitterness, at variance with her light-hearted ways, but authenticated by her factual references, has pathos and frightfulness.

"A Good Job Gone," colloquially told and fast moving, is lively and earthy. All the action points toward one vivid scene, the scuffle between Pauline and Mr. Lloyd, and economically achieves the denouement thereafter. Although the tale lacks that high seriousness often associated with permanent merit, it will probably remain popular.

Talking in July, 1961, of the source of "Red-Headed Baby," Hughes remarked: "The background was from my own merchant marine days, and those dreary ports that coastwise ships go into; and they make several trips to the same port. A sailor could very well be the father of a child." This story, the second written in Carmel and finished in September, 1933,[3] first appeared in *The Ways of White Folks.* It tells the brief visit of the red-headed sailor, Clarence, from his tramp steamer to the Florida hut of Betsy, the colored girl he had enjoyed for a price three years before. While drinking with the now experienced girl and her mother, Clarence is nonplussed by the sight of what he characterizes as "a damn runt of a red-headed baby," who turns out to be a deaf mute named Clarence. Vexed by the stares of the nearby child, the sailor leaves abruptly, violently.

This tale of careless, destructive love is told almost completely through the fragmented thoughts of "the father" Clarence. That interracial lovemaking is a regional custom is indicated by his reflections ("Holy Jesus, the yellow wenches I've had") and by the fact that two of the three Negro characters have white fathers. The author discloses his own attitude in his portrait of the child, whose severe physical handicap symbolizes the perversion of love and respect that conceived him. And he pictures the sailor as an insensitive father who recognizes his paternity with scorn and curses, who quickly seizes a violent comparison to individualize his son: "looking like one of those goggly-eyed dolls you hit with a ball at the County Fair."

"Red-Headed Baby" has one uniqueness: its stream-of-consciousness passages. Twenty-eight years passed before Hughes tried this device again in "Blessed Assurance," a story drafted eight times in 1961 and published as "Du, Meine Zuversicht" in Hamburg's *Konkret* (January, 1962) before its appearance, after being revised six more times,[4] in his collection *Something in Common and Other Stories* (1963). Of three such passages in "Red-Headed Baby," the last one reveals the sailor's thoughts before he brusquely leaves the shack: "Knocking over glasses by the oil lamp on the table where the night flies flutter Florida where skeleton houses left over from boom sand in the road and no lights in the nigger section across the railroad's knocking over glasses at edge of town where a moon-colored girl's got a red-headed baby deaf as a post like the dolls you wham at three shots for a quarter in the County Fair half full of licker and can't hit nothing." And in "Blessed Assurance," the first of two passages explores a father's anguished doubts about his son's masculinity: "He wondered vaguely with a sick feeling in his stomach should he think it through then then think it through right then through should he try then and think it through should without blacking through think blacking out then and there think it through?"

Hughes's experimental uses of interior monologue indicate by their very sparsity—and despite their appropriateness in context— that he never found the technique sufficiently natural to his mode of creation. His typical sentence fragments, also present in both stories, attempt equal service. At any rate, "Red-Headed Baby" gives play to Hughes's flair for humor in the confusion of racial etiquette caused by the Negro women's authoritative use of the first name shared by father and child. The story has social significance, and it has a favorite place in the regard of its author.

The next story has a quietness and a pathos lacking in the sexual ramblings of Mr. Lloyd and the sailor. In "Little Dog," the Negro janitor is drawn from Hughes's memory of his stepfather, Homer Clark, who was worn down by Cleveland steel mills until janitorial work was more suitable. Verifying this source in July, 1961, the author said: "Occasionally white women made passes at him. The janitor-tenant relationship is not untrue to life." In "Little Dog," written in Carmel in December, 1933,[5] and used in *The Ways of White Folks,* Clara Briggs, a middle-aged white spinster, buys a pup to fend off increasing loneliness. After two years, Joe, a Negro, becomes the new janitor in her Chicago apartment building and inherits the job of bringing meat to Flips. Ordinary civil remarks and unconscious snatches of song on Joe's part produce all the symptoms of young love in Miss Briggs, who, anticipating disruption of her tidy, detached life, moves away. Among those left behind, she incurs what always follows one who is odd without being friendly: oblivion.

Hughes's task in this third-person story was formidable. The imagination must struggle to picture a confirmed spinster crossing that no man's land fringing her lifelong ambit. And only a vigorous fancy can capture such a one crossing the American color line. Yet Hughes has Miss Briggs almost take the step without exposing her to ridicule or scorn. The story portrays, one might demur, not interracial love, but a season of irrational whim in the fading life of a lonely woman. But love can be as little— or as much, if estimated in the measure of one who has lived without it. Hughes wisely restricts the janitor's knowledge. His knowing—and possibly not fully esteeming—the woman's emotions would have injured the delicacy of a thing half hoarded and not quite savored. Her secret flurries and palpitations have the pathos of wasted love.

The characterization of the old maid distinguishes this story. Hughes makes use of what could just as easily have been a hindrance: the reader's ready-made assumptions. He profits from the stereotype by adding personal idiosyncrasies, wisps out of her past, and odd little patches in her consciousness that make her queer Miss Briggs with the dog, and nobody else. Her queerness is specific, explainable in unhackneyed terms, yet not so anatomized that the reader is certain how decisive a role Joe's race plays in her actions. That withholding of neat certitude constrains the reader to ponder the limited meaning of color.

The author's chief means of bringing the spinster to life (seen in three out of every eight passages of characterization) is to picture her responding emotionally to people and events. Only one passage in forty-six shows her effect on other people. These figures mean that the reader is made to feel with Miss Briggs as her tight little world excitingly expands, to watch her poignantly awkward attempts to adjust to it, and to understand her attitudes that will forever preclude more companionship than that obtainable from a little dog.

The question—literary, not psychological—of how the old maid falls in love with a Negro janitor is managed thoughtfully. Isolated from full life, and vulnerable to the quixotic lapses possible in her state, Miss Briggs is probably unpreoccupied with norms proscribing intimacy across the color line, or is unaware of her subconscious physical desire. She finds society only in the small amenities of two elderly colored waiters at the Rose Bud Tea Shoppe. Their daily greetings and their thoughtfulness in having special dishes prepared for her when she feels ill match the gentility and sureness about life she immediately senses in the janitor, "big and brown and kind looking," and named Joe, like one of the waiters. This daily emotional claim upon her constitutes over half of her life away from her co-workers, from whom she keeps her distance.

Miss Briggs's brief climactic scene is affecting. Her fancy lets her nobly give up her "lover" and arbitrarily refuse his advances: "She was sure he was happy down there with his portly yellow wife and his house full of children. Let him stay. . . . She never wanted to see him again, never." Her planned farewell consists of her pleasantly giving him a tip "to remember her by." It spends itself in three innocuous exchanges between the two. Joe disappears without realizing the drama in which he has starred, and "Miss Briggs slowly turned her back, shut the door, and . . . suddenly she began to cry." So ends the romance of Miss Briggs, who has always minded her own business and been cautious enough not to trust people, and whose mother once said of this girl schooled in pride, "Men'll have a hard time getting Clara."

"Little Dog" is delicate and thorough in both conception and development. It temperately criticizes a waste of life without showing disrespect for the integrity and high standards, however mistakenly conceived, that guide such an existence. Extra sadness and irony issue from the use of Negro characters, whose functions demand no racial identification, even though color augments the wistfulness of the circumstances.

The final story, "Mother and Child," is specific in origin. In September, 1960, the author said: "This was an actual situation that I turned into a conversational short story . . . a Negro farmer had a child by a white woman. There was talk in the community. The boy would be in his twenties now. He is still in the community right now as far as I know." Composed in Moscow in March, 1933,[6] and published in *The Ways of White Folks,* "Mother and Child" consists wholly of gossip among Negro women at an Ohio missionary society meeting. They talk of Douglass Carter's romance with a white girl and of the town's revenge, mainly economic, on Negro citizens. The love affair has a sincerity lacking in the other two stories of reciprocal passion; its briefly idyllic charm is revealed by two gossipers: " 'Honey, don't you know? Colored folks knowed Douglass been eyeing that woman since God knows when, and she been eyeing back at him. You ought to seed 'em when they meet in de store. Course they didn't speak no more'n Howdy, but their eyes followed one another 'round just like dogs.' "

The author's midwifery opens the story with an unseen but crying infant, whose very existence is a "shame" because it collapses twenty-two years of racial amity and transforms the white citizens into "a pack o' wolves." The Madonna-like title of the story, then, wreaks unexpected irony in the first dozen lines. This tale of the young versus the old, of love versus fear and hatred, is the only dialect story in *The Ways of White Folks*. "I was thinking of a little play or sketch," Hughes said of it in July, 1961, "but it didn't have enough plot, so I just used it as a story."

The form suits rural women at an infrequent meeting, and the dialect seems authentic and clear; but it is more useful to note what the "Poet Laureate of the Negro People" says about an emotionally explosive subject directly involving his race. His attitude is apparently expressed by a gossip at the end of these remarks about the lovers:

> "A white hussy!"
> "He's foolin' with fire."
> "Poor Mis' Carter. I'm sorry for his mother."
> "Poor Mis' Carter."
> "Why don't you all say poor Douglass? Poor white woman? Poor child?"

Hughes's regard for lovers does not pause at the color line. His reverence for life trains his eye hopefully on the young, the individual. Historical reflections in the story are strict (as straight a line can be drawn between indiscriminate economic reprisals in Ohio here and the birth pangs of Tennessee's "Tent City" of the 1960's as between the chapter "The Quarter" in Kennedy's *Swallow Barn* of 1832 and today's strictures against Negroes). But the story's implied concentration on the future and the possibilities of individual contributions to it, when added to the tale's refrain, "they was in love," shows the appeal of the love story to Hughes—and points ahead to "Cora Unashamed."

II *Life Beyond Color*

Among his ten poems read at the National Poetry Festival at the Library of Congress on October 24, 1962, Hughes included "Border Line":

> I used to wonder
> About living and dying—
> I think the difference lies
> Between tears and crying.
>
> I used to wonder
> About here and there—
> I think the distance
> Is nowhere.

"A poem, I think," he told the audience, "should be the distilled essence of an emotion—the shorter the better." His practice of this view is more evident in his nonracial than in his racial poetry. A fitting coincidence attaches to the proportion of these two broad categories in Hughes's poems: whereas every tenth person in America has been said to be Negro, roughly every tenth poem by Hughes has no reference to color.

"Border Line," in *Fields of Wonder* (1947), probably had its emotional birth in December, 1937, in the French village of Tour de Carol, just across the border from war-embattled Spain. The final pages of *I Wonder* record Hughes's thoughts as he sat in the station buffet: "What a difference a border makes: on one side of an invisible line, food; on the other side, none. On one side, peace. On the other side, war." At least seven years before, "Aesthete in Harlem" had touched upon this universal feeling (which might well be named "the exhilaration of the boundary line"), common to experiences as diverse as Hughes's leaving Mexico in 1921 and Thoreau's entering Walden in 1845. The "distilled essence" aimed at by Hughes in this poem is remarkably captured in the third and fourth lines. They are the emotional heart of the poem, and it is superior to its intellectual point, made in the final two lines.

The author's nonracial poetic themes number no more than twenty, and brief references to several indicate the quality of his efforts. Like all poets who write much, Hughes writes of death. Among his competent early poems are "Death of an Old Seaman" and "To a Little Lover-Lass, Dead"—*Vanity Fair* took both in 1925—each quietly sentimental and marked by some original phrasing. A third poem, "Dear Lovely Death," appeared in *Opportunity* in June, 1930, before becoming the title piece of a fourteen-page, privately printed volume the following year. The poem adds cosmic beneficence to death, matched by a wide view of "this suffering flesh." A few poems on death are sad, but most of them range through natural acceptance, defiance, and even humor.

About one-fourth of the nonracial poems treat nature. Typically, they contain vivid impressions of the moon, the sea, the seasons, or some natural phenomenon brought near to human life. His best nature poems are visual pictures, like "Winter Moon" (*The Crisis*, August, 1923): "How thin and sharp is the moon tonight!/How thin and sharp and ghostly white/Is the slim curved crook of the moon tonight!" His sea poems reveal little more than an imaginative landsman's view of that repository of mystery. The six-line "Sea Calm," in *The Weary Blues* (1926), needs as its second half some uneasy feeling of a sailor at sea, not the temporary recoil of a stroller on an Eastern boardwalk; of the "strangely still" water, the poet merely says that "It is not good/For water/To be so still that way."

Some early nature poems are spoiled by sentimental person-ifications, such as the naked moon that does not blush in "March Moon." Shock, followed by gradual admiration like that roused by some seventeenth-century metaphysical poets, accompanies the opening lines of "Caribbean Sunset": "God having a hem-orrhage,/Blood coughed across the sky." Both poems appeared in *The Weary Blues*. The nature poems are generally com-petent, but not brilliant. Confined largely to the beginning and middle portions of his career, they form a substantial pattern in the wide-based spiral of his developing art.

Bigger than nature is life, and life to Hughes has been a "big sea" fished with gratitude. His poetry shows this acceptance of mankind. "Mexican Market Woman" (*The Crisis*, March, 1922) pictures an "ancient hag" seated on the ground. But the teen-age poet says she "has known high wind-swept mountains./ And the sun has made/Her skin so brown." The poem shows respect for human nature and for the artist's role in preserving its beauty. "Daybreak in Alabama" (in *Unquote*, June, 1940), titled after the song the young speaker is dreaming he will compose some day, bespeaks a love for people. The middle portion describes the contents of the song: the scent of pine and red clay; "long red necks," "poppy colored faces";

> And the field daisy eyes
> Of black and white black white black people
> And I'm gonna put white hands
> And black hands and brown and yellow hands
> And red clay earth hands in it
> Touching everybody with kind fingers.

Hughes's lyrical hope for America fuses natural color and fragrance in objects and people, transformed by the "kind fingers" of creative love.

Life, love, and joy blow a clean wind of optimism through much of Hughes's poetry. In "Mama and Daughter," in *One-Way*

Ticket, a mother, while brushing the coat of her daughter who is going out to meet her "sugar-sweet," lets the girl know that she once followed the same normal impulse. In "Harlem Night Song," in *The Weary Blues,* romantic love shapes the ghetto into moonlit roof-tops and turns cabaret jazz into an echo for two singing evening strollers. Natural joy and simple earthiness pervade the poem "Joy" (in *The Crisis,* February, 1926). The protagonist, looking for "Slim, dancing Joy,/Gay, laughing Joy," finds her "Driving the butcher's cart/In the arms of the butcher boy!" But "Passing Love" (in *Opportunity,* March, 1927) modifies, through the reminder of its transience, the joy that love brings. It begins:

> Because you are to me a song
> I must not sing you over-long.
> Because you are to me a prayer
> I cannot say you everywhere.

Some love poetry is conventional or sentimental, such as the very early "Ardella" and "A Black Pierrot," both in *The Weary Blues;* some later pieces, like "Desire" and "Sleep" in *Fields of Wonder,* are frank but restrained pictures of physical love. In the latter volume, Hughes's variously expressed insistence on the permanent value of life appears in "Walls," and more particularly in "Girl," whose protagonist dies after a life of "sinful happiness." But, from her coffin in the earth, "Seems like she said:/*My body/ Brings new birth.*"

Through Hughes's use of dreams, as ductile to young poets as love, his spiral progression through sentimentalism, sturdy faith, and social criticism is traceable. The evolution is clearly not linear, for "Dreams" (in *The World Tomorrow,* 1923) is not merely sentimental. It starts:

> Hold fast to dreams
> For if dreams die
> Life is a broken-winged bird
> That cannot fly.

On the other hand, "I Dream a World" (in *Teamwork,* February, 1945—and afterwards published in perhaps fifty other places, Hughes estimates) is more sentimental in its expectations, despite its strong social criticism. After its midpoint, it continues:

A world I dream where black or white,
Whatever race you be,
Will share the bounties of the earth
And every man is free, . . .

Poems of hope are, and ought to be, popular among a writer's followers when written with compelling imagination and sincerity. "Youth," in *The Crisis* in August, 1924, and titled simply "Poem" in *The Weary Blues*, meets those standards. As popular as "I Dream a World," it begins with "We have tomorrow/ Bright before us/Like a flame," and ends with optimistic attention on "dawn today/Broad arch above the road we came." "Freedom's Plow" tells in seven pages the importance of vision ("First in the heart is the dream"); of creative cooperation ("labor—white hands and black hands"); of faith in the public ("The people often hold/Great thoughts in their deepest hearts"); and of broad perspective ("That plow plowed a new furrow/Across the field of history").

Hughes's stories as often as his poems have little to do with race. At least nine—exclusive of several sketches and humorous narratives—of the sixty-six that he has published belong in this category. "Cora Unashamed" and "On the Way Home" are distinctly superior to the others. *I Wonder* tells the setting of the writing of the former in the New Moscow Hotel. It was the aftermath of Hughes's reading two stories by D. H. Lawrence that had brought "cold sweat and goose pimples" to his body:

> A night or two after . . . I sat down to write an *Izvestia* article on Tashkent when, instead, I began to write a short story. I had been saying to myself all day, "If D. H. Lawrence can write such psychologically powerful accounts of folks in England . . . maybe I could write stories like his about folks in America. . . .
>
> . . . I began to think about some of the people in my own life, and some of the tales I had heard from others, that affected me in the same hair-raising manner. . . . I began to turn over in my mind a story that a young lawyer in California, Loren Miller, had told me. . . .

In 1960 Hughes reminisced, talking about details of the story: "In the town where [Miller] lived, . . . there was one Negro doctor and one Negro undertaker and one Negro minister. The prettiest girl in the town got pregnant. The gossip was that she had been going with all three. Her mother took her for an abortion to Kansas City and she died. The minister preached the funeral, the undertaker performed the burial, and the doctor was there. The whole town turned out to see what would happen. Nothing happened." The autobiography tells his transformation of his material: "When I sat down at my well-traveled type-writer and began to write my first short story, 'Cora Unashamed,' . . . the Negro girl became a white girl . . . whose parents did not want her to fall in love with an immigrant Greek boy. . . . My story consisted of what happened when this girl's mother forced her to have an abortion, the girl died, and the Negro cook spoke her piece. . . ." After talking of these changes in September, 1960, Hughes remarked, "It seemed a pity to me that a girl should have to die just for that."

The author's written and oral explanations are quoted because of their pertinence to one of his best stories and because of their revelation of his creative processes. He began to write almost involuntarily, desiring to turn out stories of psychological in-tensity, and he held that his *story consisted of* the dramatically human moments of the action. The author's feeling that the climax was "a pity" shows that the trap door of sentimentality lay open. One factual reference is questionable: his naming this narrative his "first short story." "Mary Winosky" and the West Illana Series preceded it, of course; but, more pertinent, Hughes's own recently located list of stories shows four written in the hotel before this one.[7]

Written in April and published in September, 1933, by *The American Mercury* (which also accepted "Poor Little Black Fellow" in May),[8] this story presents Cora Jenkins, the cook and maid for twenty-seven of her forty years for the Studevant family of Melton, Iowa. The one lover in Cora's past, a foreign boy named Joe, left town when she became pregnant with a girl who soon died. Transferring her love to Jessie, newly born to Mrs. Studevant, Cora sheltered the growing child for years against an indifferent family ashamed of Jessie's dull placidness. But the girl, not too dull to turn outside the family for solace, be-comes pregnant by Willie Matsoulos. An "Easter shopping trip" to Kansas City for Jessie is her mother's remedy. After the girl dies from the abortion, Cora addresses the coffined body at the funeral, screaming:

"They killed you! And for nothin'. . . . They took you . . . in the
Springtime of your life, and now you'se gone, gone!"

Folks were paralyzed in their seats.

Cora went on: "They preaches you a pretty sermon and they
don't say nothin'. They sings you a song, and they don't say
nothin'. But Cora's . . . gonna tell 'em why they took you to
Kansas City."

Strong Studevant arms rush her into the back yard. Later she
leaves the family for good, moving with her parents to the edge
of town.

Both carnal and parental love are ingloriously defeated. The
fleshly love of Cora and Jessie for their paramours is made gross
by desertion or made hapless by nullification and punishment.
Cora's familial love binds her to semi-ignorance and lifelong
drudgery. Her love for her own child is snuffed out at the edge
of a tiny grave. Jessie's parents are too mired in work, petty civic
ambitions, and false pride to love her; their lives tangle with hers
only in alienating spankings or reprimands. Jessie's unborn child,
which would have brought love into her thin existence, is
sacrificed to callous selfishness.

Illegitimacy is merely ancillary to this theme, although, shortly
before writing this story, Hughes was impressed by the dilemma
of a girl from Pittsburgh: having just come to the Soviet Union
to bear her illegitimate child free of stigma, she "planted herself
in the New Moscow Hotel on a three-day permit, intending to
remain. . . ." Cora is unashamed of illegitimacy, unashamed of
life and love in their every natural expression. Hughes, con-
fronted in July, 1961, with the suggestion that "worship of life"
might describe Cora's attitude, replied: "She has willing and
joyous acceptance of life. 'Worship' implies a greater consciousness on her part of what she is thinking. 'Worship' seems
planned."

The author skillfully characterizes Cora. He pictures her early
as "an inoffensive soul, except that she sometimes cussed,"
establishing credibility for her later outbursts of profanity—as in
Vardis Fisher's "Laughter," a story that successfully presents a
bishop cursing during his funeral eulogy. The reader's dual view
of Cora, "humble in the face of life," "not humble before the
fact of death," full of love or of raging protest as her simple
nature may demand, lets him anticipate her two major responses
and judge morally her bipolar attitudes. She almost walks on life

and death, like Melville's Ahab—though the comparison is limited.

Cora adds human strength to the symbolic texture of the story. Like a tree, "once rooted, she stood, in spite of storms and strife, wind, and rocks, in the earth." Uncomplicated herself, she makes life simpler for Jessie; she aligns her with nature, which in this story symbolizes gentle joy, rightness, life itself. The Studevant house, the entire town in fact, is isolated from nature. The orchard and green fields beyond which Cora's little Josephine lies buried are "at the edge of Melton."

The town and family environment seems hostile to nature in other ways. In what the author calls "Cora's springtime," Josephine is born illegitimately and removed in pain; in Jessie's figurative and actual last springtime, intolerance snatches away her child's life and her own. The funeral garlands over which the Studevant men stumble to quash the truth on the maid's lips are like nature rising to claim for one of its adherents the right to be heard. At the end of the story, Cora and her parents cultivate their little garden "on the edge of Melton." Their garden, like the planted flowers of spring, lies halfway between the man-made and the natural worlds. Like Candide, Cunegonde, Pangloss, and Martin, the worn-out Jenkins family accepts the only compromise that integrity allows: hard work within the circle of mankind, but outside the miasma of its low designs.

The variety of style in this third-person narrative merits more attention than space allows: elasticity in diction, adaptation of sentence length to intended effect, and audience-involving devices of the raconteur. Asked about the last technique in July, 1961, Hughes said, "I don't consciously think of myself as . . . telling a story to listeners." Two racial themes are briefly reflected: the blindness inflicted by suppositions framed wholly on color (Cora comforts weeping Jessie with: "And there ain't no reason why you can't marry, neither—you both white"); and the social vacuum suffocating Negro youngsters in many small towns (Cora's brothers left Melton because of sheer loneliness; her sisters left because of sexual exploitation by whites).

Using less irony than usual, and little humor, in this work that appeared in O'Brien's *Best Short Stories of 1934*, Hughes scarcely betrays the sentimentality in his view of Miller's story. It vanishes into the maid's funeral tirade and angry blasphemy as she turns from the grave of her child (whose death and burial receive only three lines): "She cussed out God for taking away the life that she herself had given. She screamed, 'My baby! God damn it! My baby! I bear her and you take her away!' She looked at the sky . . . and yelled in defiance." Cora is too strong for pathos to color her existence; and the sorrow that would touch the harmed or stolen lives of those she loves somehow withers before the spirited profanity with which she denounces the subjection of love and innocent will to callous forces.

The author spoke of "On the Way Home" in September, 1960, as follows: "There is a factual basis. But I don't quite place the character. Somebody's mother died . . . so they went home. I've known two or three people who in the presence of death go to pieces in a drunken way and think they're having a good time." First entitled "The Bottle of Wine," the story was written some-time in 1941[9] and first appeared in *Story* for May-June, 1946. The narrative shows the movements of young Carl Anderson of Chicago after he receives a telegram from neighbors of his loving mother in Sommerville telling of her critical illness. Model-ing his actions on men in novels, the teetotaler hurries to his room with a bottle of wine. As he drinks, perspires, prays, and readies himself for a bus ride home, he thinks of his loneliness, his bills for his mother and himself. He composes a song about spring and roses, remembering how he has been financially un-able to take girls out. Having emptied the bottle, he sings lustily in his bath, imagining himself owning a car and riding with girls. After several hours of drunken sleep in his room, he receives a telephone call saying his mother has just died. He rushes to the corner tavern for the first time in his life, orders "a drink," and permits the advances of a woman at the bar. Her suggestions unnerve him, through her repeated references to "home," until he begins to cry.

In this story, Carl Anderson's all the way, three out of every five passages characterizing him explore his emotional reactions to his tepid past, empty present, and supposedly redemptive future. Hughes's aim, then, is a dramatic analysis of the winged life which maternal love has folded in a sheath of dead habit. Carl's disappearing past spells one word, "mother"; means one mood, her kindness; and is replaceable only by the disenchant-ment that her "Be good, Be clean, and Be sweet" are not in-scribed on the face of nature.

Carl's every act, once the telegram comes, reveals ambivalence toward his mother. The alienation grows. He rushes up the stairs to his room, an act not consonant with the anxious sorrow of a man who must wait three hours for a bus. Now and then Hughes shows Carl aware of his ambivalence, as when, standing tall with song in the bathtub, he answers Mrs. Dyer's imperious knock and query (ellipses are Hughes's):

> "I'm on the way home to see my mother. She. . . ."
> "You sound happier than a lark about it. I couldn't imagine. . . ."
> He heard the landlady's feet shuffling [away].
> "She's. . . ." His head began to go round and round.

The reader surely breathes the word "dying" to Carl, who cannot damn himself and his floating cheer. Hughes spares him with drunkenness, but only after the lees of truth have been stirred up from filial piety. A certain headlong frankness proceeds from the wine: a gift for his mother would be useless, he decides; and his manner on the telephone (his quadruple "Yes, Mrs. Rossiter") is prompting, not apprehensive.

Motherly love has stifled Carl's manliness. To this novel-reading teetotaler, the phrase wine-women-and-song must be as delectable as the warm bath. His private song, "When the roses sing/In the spring," and his intense recall of his mother's breaking up his games with a little girl on a grassy slope match his daydreams and subconscious resentments. The image-making qualities of wine and water are toned by Hughes to Carl's recollection, to his anticipation of feminine solace; and they are finally concentrated in a woman's voice. Eight times the images of wine and water are sweet, warm, forbidden, easy; they invest the texture of Carl's body in the bath, the pillow in which he quiets his mother's voice and buries his new song. The prostitute solicits him in a "warm low voice" and purrs gently. But she cracks the mirror in which he is forming his new image by dallying with "baby" and "little boy."

Hughes upholds the basic sincerity of Carl's love for his mother. (His forgotten father had been a drunkard.) His quick prayer for her as he uncorks the wine bottle and his fear as he considers packing a dark suit are genuine. Rushing toward the bar, the environs of his newborn liberty sensed in the bathtub ritual—itself a half-realized rebirth—Carl is gnawed by an insistent question that dries his throat: *"Alone, at home, alone!"*

and "*Did she die alone?*" His sobs at the bar awake undeniable memories of a home that, after all, had given him a mother's love.

"On the Way Home," narrated in the third person, has delicacy of understanding and a psychologically even perception of character and motivation. It is a story, not of a man on the way home, but of a man whom death brings painfully into the world a second time, in a rebirth made necessary by a superfluity of maternal love.

A curious and revealing bit of history attended publication of this story. Study of Hughes's various autographed inscriptions on drafts in his files and at Yale, and examination of correspondence between Whit Burnett of *Story* and Hughes's agent, Maxim Lieber, shows the following facts. From the time of composition at Hollow Hills Farm in 1941 through revisions in Chicago and Milwaukee to July 27, 1945, the prostitute was blonde. The next day, Hughes changed her to "brownskin" at the request of the staff of *Story*. Hughes filed the altered pages 9 and 10 as an alternative-ending appendage; and by the time "On the Way Home" appeared in the 1952 collection, the woman had no skin color at all.

Beguiling nuances of attitude appear in the correspondence, but it suffices to observe that racial identification of the prostitute is meaningless, especially since one cannot investigate the races of Carl and his landlady, not to mention his parents. This peculiar issue Hughes remembered first of all, when talking about the story in September, 1960: "This is the one," he smiled, "that Whit Burnett wrote me about, asking whether it was a colored story or white story. He asked if the woman who picked [Carl] up at the bar was colored." The author's note on the cover sheet of six copies of variously revised pages 9 and 10 at Yale ends thus: "I am afraid many American white/people have a color complex, even/editors."

Other relevant stories—"Tragedy at the Baths," "Little Old Spy," "Mysterious Madame Shanghai," "Thank You, M'am," "Sorrow for a Midget," "His Last Affair," and "Never Room with a Couple"—are entertaining, extending the settings to New York, Mexico, and Cuba. They add melodrama, international intrigue, adventure, sentiment, and individual pathos. They include the tall tale and the domestic tragedy. They show Hughes's concern for ordinary people made significant by their varieties of strength, or saved from insignificance by the light he throws upon them.

III   *Negro Soul*

"To [intercultural national themes] the Negro artist can give his racial individuality, his heritage of rhythm and warmth, and his incongruous humor that so often, as in the Blues, becomes ironic laughter mixed with tears. . . . ." This portion of the life-long manifesto of Hughes, published June 23, 1926, in *The Nation* as "The Negro Artist and the Racial Mountain," is followed by his prediction that Negro artists will rise and thrive, will show "their own soul-world." Confident that full expression of the Negro soul-world would be a precious addition to the main-stream of American and world culture, Hughes has often employed novel and experimental forms to achieve it.

1.   *Blues*

"My soul has grown deep like the rivers," declares Hughes in one of his earliest and most famous poems, "The Negro Speaks of Rivers." Negro soul is not a subject, but a complex of feelings (*"Yo no estudio al negro. Lo siento,"* the author told Nicolás Guillén on his second trip to Cuba in 1930). In Kansas City at the age of nine, on Independence Avenue and on Twelfth Street, Hughes was first impressed—outside family circles—by the sound of the Negro soul: He heard the blues, his first inspiration to write poetry.[10]

He undertook a difficult task when he sought to communicate the poetry of the blues through written words alone—and at a time when Bessie and Clara Smith, and Ethel Waters, were popularizing the blues with all the advantages that musical, vocal, and gestic art combine. While singing the blues, these artists, with a stiffening of the back, could suggest historical chain-gang chants to the spellbound listener; with diverting wrist, torso, or hip movements, they could lessen the potential monotony of the repeated lines; with various facial expressions, they could signal the recall of much of the spiritual beauty, or anguish, of Negro history. But the rigid blues pattern, within which vocal artists and instrumentalists were free to evoke and personalize an entire tradition, was a limitation to the poet. To give artistic expression of permanent value to a form demanding simple diction, repetition, and an elementary rhyme scheme raised problems. Examination of a few of his best blues poems shows Hughes's contribution of a new verse form to our literature.

Although the prize-winning title poem of *The Weary Blues* contains part of a blues song "coming from a black man's soul," two-thirds of the lines describe the piano player. The picture is vivid, but it is not a poetic transcription of the blues form. In 1921 Hughes mailed to *The Crisis* a striking poem closer to the required form, "Song for a Banjo Dance," which opens as follows:

> Shake your brown feet, honey,
> Shake your brown feet, chile,
> Shake your brown feet, honey,
> Shake 'em swift and wil'—
> Get way back, honey,
> Do that low-down step.
> Walk on over, darling,
> Now! Come out
> With your left.

In the prefatory pages of *Fine Clothes to the Jew*, Hughes explains: "The *Blues* . . . have a strict rhyme pattern: one long line repeated and a third line to rhyme with the first two. Sometimes the second line . . . is slightly changed and sometimes . . . it is omitted." This poem does not adhere to that pattern. Nor does it as a whole display enough of the traditional mood, which, the author's note goes on to say, "is almost always despondency, but when they are sung people laugh." Although not blues, this poem reflects the Negro soul through its spreading joy, its defiant rhythm that shakes itself at hovering melancholy.

Two works first published in 1926 are excellent examples of the blues form faithfully rendered as poetry: "Homesick Blues" (in *Literary Digest*, July 13, 1926) and "Po' Boy Blues" (in *Poetry* in November, 1926). The former, flawed by the rhyming of "have" and "laughs," opens thus:

> De railroad bridge's
> A sad song in de air.
> De railroad bridge's
> A sad song in de air.
> Ever time de trains pass
> I wants to go somewhere.

The metaphor has perfect feeling and truth; it has roll and smoke and fading song. It is high and trembling but as unspectacular as the mind responding to it. The situation, simple and complete, is that of a hobo looking for a southbound freight to carry him home.

"Po' Boy Blues" never departs from the rigid form. It begins:

> When I was home de
> Sunshine seemed like gold.
> When I was home de
> Sunshine seemed like gold.
> Since I come up North de
> Whole damn world's turned cold.

This typical stanza is followed by three more on the common themes of world-weariness and romantic troubles: the hard life not worth living and the heartless or faithless lover. The ending fuses the moods:

> Weary, weary,
> Early, early in de morn.
> I's so weary
> I wish I'd never been born.

With this best early effort at strict adherence to the form belongs "Evenin' Air Blues" (*Common Ground*, Spring, 1941), equal to any of his later productions in the genre. It begins with "Folks, I come up North/Cause they told me de North was fine"; but the first stanza ends with the speaker confessing that after six months "I'm about to lose my mind." The next stanza excellently explains laughter at sad blues:

> This mornin' for breakfast
> I chawed de mornin' air.
> This mornin' for breakfast
> Chawed de mornin' air.
> But this evenin' for supper,
> I got evenin' air to spare.

The humorous "chawed de mornin' air" seems to reflect the imagination of a semiliterate folk Negro, but it has literary parallels. Yeats, in "Among School Children," sees Maud Gonne "Hollow of cheek as though it drank the wind/And took a mess of shadows for its meat." Thoreau, in "Solitude" in *Walden,* prefers to the pills of quacks "a draught of undiluted morning air." And Emerson, in "The Transcendentalist," praises idealists as "terrible friends" who "eat clouds, and drink wind."

The hungry Negro has a meaningful remedy: "Believe I'll do a little dancin'/Just to drive my blues away"; then he tells what blues are:

> But if you was to ask me
> How de blues they come to be,
> Says if you was to ask me
> How de blues they come to be—
> You wouldn't need to ask me:
> Just look at me and see!

This superior blues poem, marred only by the rhyming of "fine" and "mind" and by dialectal inconsistency in "they" and "de," has typical contextual simplicity, humor, melancholy, and spurts of vital imagery. The final stanza, saying that the Negro's condition explains the blues, suggests that much Negro experience in and out of slavery has been transfused into folk art. Scholarship is uncovering the necessity, in the interdisciplinary examination of American culture, of a thorough study of the Negro folk tradition: spirituals, plantation, chain-gang, and levee songs; blues and jazz—to mention only some songs. Hughes's innovations in the poetry of blues and jazz will be more perceptively judged as this folk art and literature become more widely understood.

"The Blues I'm Playing" was written in September, 1933,[11] and published in *Scribner's Magazine* in May, 1934. Of its origin Hughes said in September, 1960: "This came partly out of my own experience with patrons; it was a compilation of cases of which I am aware." "This could have happened with my own patron," he added in July, 1961. "It did not happen, but it could have." The story, the first to issue from the comfort and quiet of the cottage at Carmel, tells of Oceola Jones, Harlem pianist and protégée of wealthy Dora Ellsworth, a middle-aged, childless widow interested solely in art. Mrs. Ellsworth whisks Oceola away from Harlem house parties and Pete Williams, her Pullman porter lover, and later from her mixed groups of Greenwich Village gin drinkers to an upstate mountain lodge. Trying to divest the girl's soul of jazz, Mrs. Ellsworth has her trained abroad and arranges concerts there. When both return to New York, however, the patron finds Oceola "not yet sublimated, even by Philippe," her Parisian mentor; for the girl plans to marry

Pete Williams when he graduates from college. Mrs. Ellsworth withdraws as patron. Playing for the last time in her benefactress's music room, Oceola shifts her performance abruptly to a stunning mixture of blues and jazz that makes the lilies tremble in their Persian vases. "This is mine," she explains to her patron, still playing; and she briefly tells her what blues are made of.

The relation of this story to Hughes's life and to the cult of the Negro can be passed over. Thematically, it presents a conflict between life and art—one that need not exist, Oceola's choices and actions tell us. The blues are aligned mostly with life, their source and the arbiter of their form. Art is here represented by a disciplined career devoted to old masters and old forms; life, by love and marriage and by immersion in duties to one's self and community. Art is associated with entrenched wealth; life, with youthful vigor.

Art never transcends life. Embodied in Dora Ellsworth, art merely offers from its hoard of cash the blandishments of convenience and privilege, trying to draw away life's vitality and induce it to follow the rules by which art claims its superiority. Life, in the person of Oceola Jones, sings itself in blues and jazz in Harlem, ignores artistic East 63rd Street, raises no brows at bottle-in-hand gin drinkers. In Europe, it can stretch its body between the Harlem of shouting churches and the concert halls of the Continent. In New York again, it plans to multiply itself, and life in a beautiful music room happily gives up its secret to an aging widow who no longer believes in any secrets except those of genius.

Hughes joins the portraits of Dora Ellsworth and Oceola in the way art and life must merge: one selective, one encompassing; one withdrawn, one engaged. To the widow—whose perception of genius was once dulled by the odor of garlic—Greenwich Village, a New York State mountain lodge, and the Left Bank are equidistant from her purse if they can help unburden her protégée's soul of the blues and jazz which degrade the dignity of a grand piano. The electric strength Mrs. Ellsworth sees in the "rich velvet black" body of Oceola should serve only classical music.

A personal rapport, shown in the most charming scene in the story, harmonizes thematic strains. In Oceola's little Paris apartment, the aging white woman tells romantic tales of old France and, out of her childhood love, sings simple French tunes her

husband never tried to understand. The two sing together, and
Mrs. Ellsworth ventures to sing spirituals. Loneliness and un-
appreciated sensitivity, then, have wrought in this austere woman
the certainty that what she lost—"a beautiful life"—can be found
only in art, art so good that it is better than most life, and better,
therefore, than most people. Hughes at twenty-one knew that
this concept was not true; he tossed one form of art—his books—
into the sea.

The closeness of the blues to sensory life appears in the un-
forced selectivity of Oceola's mind as she summarizes her past
for her patron. She remembers Mobile's delicious roast pig and
the large mouth of Billy Kersands, the minstrel leader who let her
as a child place both hands inside it. The relevance of Negro experience to blues and jazz is the point in her recollection that her
parents, both musicians, were run out of town for being dressed
up in Alabama. Happy playing either blues or classics, she
cannot "stare mystically over the top of a grand piano like white
folks and imagine that Beethoven had nothing to do with life."

The last few pages of the story deserve close study. In them
Oceola answers her patron's final argument, much used against
the young: "You don't know, child, what men are like." The
answer, a defense of life against art, is in the lilies trembling
before the tomtom beat of blues. The answer is the fact that Mrs.
Ellsworth, dressed in a gown of black velvet and a collar of
pearls—a symbolic fusion of herself and her protégée—still looks
"very cold and white." While the widow decries Oceola's preference for a man rather than greatness, the pianist responds with
"the soft and lazy syncopation of a Negro blues. . . ."

Oceola's final words, chartable according to mood, race, and
sex, explain what blues are [ellipses are Hughes's]: "'Listen!
. . . How sad and gay it is. Blue and happy—laughing and crying. . . . How white like you and black like me. . . . How much
like a man. . . . And how like a woman. . . . Warm as Pete's
mouth. . . . These are the blues. . . . I'm playing.'"

Every word and deed of both characters in this well-con-
structed, third-person story adds to the give-and-take. The
women, symbolic but also individual, show in their moments of
sympathy, days of workmanlike cooperation, and times of collision the beneficial jostling of life and art. Oceola, church
worker, blues and jazz enthusiast, lover, and concert artist, keeps
her fingers on the keyboard of life. Like the folk Negro protag-

onist of "Evenin' Air Blues," she sees the secret of the blues in her own life, and the truth of her expression will not be compromised. Her story shows that man's art is more viable because the Oceolas and the Dora Ellsworths do not worship at the same temple.

2. *Jazz*

In the "black and laughing, heartbreaking blues" and jazz of Paris dawns in 1924, as Hughes describes them in *The Big Sea*, the young poet found his first prolonged incentive to turn jazz into poetry. Music at the Grand Duc obviously inspired "To a Negro Jazz Band in a Parisian Cabaret," in *The Crisis*, December, 1925; but the source of his earliest jazz poem of unquestionable merit, "Jazzonia" (*The Crisis*, August, 1923), is less definite. At all times after leaving Mexico in 1921, however, Hughes responded to the music which lent its name to the decade.

> Oh, silver tree!
> Oh, shining rivers of the soul!
>
> In a Harlem cabaret
> Six long-headed jazzers play.
> A dancing girl whose eyes are bold
> Lifts high a dress of silken gold.
>
> Oh, singing tree!
> Oh, shining rivers of the soul!

This is the first half of "Jazzonia," a poem apparently written a little after "The Weary Blues," and one of the three shown Vachel Lindsay. It opens with an ecstatic union of sensory and spiritual faculties, with vocalic suggestions both rapturous and solemn. The next stanza gives dual recognition to the exotic thrust of jazz: its then strange extravagance is drawn with cubist sharpness, but kept expressively realistic, through the Picasso-like image of the jazz men's six long heads massed and tilted. Its sexuality is colorfully emphatic in the enticing dancing girl. Allusions to Eve and Cleopatra add depth to the theme of allurement; and several interchanges of adjectives before "tree" and "rivers" fuse the reader's perceptions in apt anticipation of the concluding lines: "In a whirling cabaret/Six long-headed jazzers play."

The other poem that impressed Vachel Lindsay, "Negro Dancers," appeared in *The Crisis* in March, 1925. Its vigor and rhythmical exactness are fully represented by the opening stanza, spoken thus:

> "Me an' ma baby's
> Got two mo' ways,
> Two mo' ways to do de Charleston!"
> Da, da,
> Da, da, da!
> Two mo' ways to do de Charleston!"

After a second stanza on the cabaret atmosphere of the "brown-skin steppers," and a third that reads like two snaps of the thumb at white onlookers, the poem ends with a repetition of the opening three lines. Except for the second stanza, the poem is notable for its precise rendition of the dance that captured the verve, speed, and abandon of the Jazz Age and enthralled Paris in the persons of many Negro dancers, especially Josephine Baker.

"Lenox Avenue: Midnight," the next published in the series of Hughes's best jazz pieces, appeared in *The Weary Blues.* Recorded as the expressions of a Negro woman, it partially explains jazz: "The rhythm of life/Is a jazz rhythm." The second stanza indicates that jazz, like rain and street sounds, can vaguely mirror human woes. The final stanza, because of its tight rhythmical pattern and dramatic intimations, suggests movement by the speaker into a slow jazz step:

> Lenox Avenue,
> Honey.
> Midnight,
> And the gods are laughing at us.

This poem, a softly finger-popping affirmation of life that makes the laughter of the gods somewhat irrelevant, survives the effect of its middle, which reflects a rather different consciousness and speech.

"Negro Servant," mentioned in Chapter III, adds a picture of jazz as "drums of life in Harlem after dark!" and salutes the music with "O, dreams!/ O, songs!/O, saxophones at night!" Elsewhere the poem evokes memories of African drums and veldt. Jazz is the after-hours music of oppressed people ("O, songs that do not care!"), a repository of dreams and half-buried recollections of a vibrant culture once theirs.

The meaning of jazz to the musician is combined with racial

background in "Trumpet Player" in *Fields of Wonder*. Jazz is "honey/Mixed with liquid fire"; and the trumpet player, says the poet at the end, never knows "Upon what riff the music slips/Its hypodermic needle/To his soul." Finally, to the musician, trouble "Mellows to a golden note." The first third of the poem outlines the Negro musician, tired eyes smoldering with memories of slavery, hair "tamed down." The weakest stanza shows the Negro's longing for the moon and sea as "old desire" distilled into rhythm. The quoted lines and a few others reveal the true distillation, jazz made precious by its long and sacrificial birth.

While writing "Trumpet Player," Hughes was fully abreast of the new be-bop music emerging from Minton's Playhouse in Harlem. Among the poems inspired by be-bop—a rhythmically complex and experimental kind of jazz characterized by dissonance, improvisation, and unusual lyrics—the best is the lead-off "Dream Boogie" in *Montage of a Dream Deferred* (1951):

> Good morning, daddy!
> Ain't you heard
> The boogie-woogie rumble
> Of a dream deferred?
>
> Listen closely:
> You'll hear their feet
> Beating out and beating out a—
>
> > *You think*
> > *It's a happy beat?*
>
> Listen to it closely:
> Ain't you heard
> something underneath
> like a—
>
> > *What did I say?*
>
> Sure,
> I'm happy!
> Take it away!
>
> > *Hey, pop!*
> > *Re-bop!*
> > *Mop!*
>
> > *Y-e-a-h!*

Keeping up with a changing Harlem, Hughes is alert to the "hip" insider's elastic jargon as well as the generations-old truth of Negro life—the dream deferred. "Dream Boogie" perfectly fulfills its purpose, wasting no word. It has variation in mood: ease, irony, sarcasm, and terse joviality. It mixes old devices of the dramatic monologue with a contemporary boogiewoogie beat. Its rough-hewn grace adds power to its clarity.

Jazz poems can reveal jazz even less than blues poems can reveal the blues: the strict form of the latter provides some agreement between poet and reader. Yet, followers of Bud Powell, Dizzy Gillespie, Thelonious Monk, and Charlie Parker can respond with extra enthusiasm and sureness to the be-bop and jazz poems. In the public alliance of poetry and music so challenging in the case of jazz poems, Hughes has been a pioneer. On October 7, 1958, he told Harry Elliott of the Lawrence, Kansas, *Journal-World:* "I did poetry reading with a jazz piano, including . . . Fats Waller, in Harlem friends' homes in the early 1920's." His reading to glee-club music at Princeton in 1928 was part of a more public tradition that he was firmly establishing by then. The Greenwich Village and San Francisco Beat Movement of the late 1950's was an extravagant development of Hughes's lead.

If, in his evolution as a poet shown in his 1951 volume, Hughes was restricting himself to folk material and to experimental and folk art methods (a warning mixed with praise in reviews by Saunders Redding in *New York Herald Tribune Book Review,* March 11, 1951, and by Babette Deutsch in *The New York Times Book Review,* May 6, 1951), the restriction was purposeful. Restriction is the subject of the blues, the fountainhead of jazz, and the tuning fork of the Negro soul. A true blues or jazz poem is an expression of this very restriction, modified by intimations of how Negroes transcend it. "Believe I'll do a little dancin'/Just to drive my blues away" and "Oh, silver tree!/Oh, shining rivers of the soul!" are exact reflections of Negro soul: its supple power to overcome demoralization, its gift of recognizing the flow of spirit inside kindred forms. To be true, the intellectual content of such poems must be aborted: the lazy stomp of a jazz step and the sudden "Hey, pop!/Re-bop!" interrupt and squash thought and reason in an irrational world of color prejudice. For the folk Negro, to think is not to be.

3. *Negritude*

The Negroes' "own soul-world" that centralized Hughes's purposes in the 1920's is the American counterpart of the burgeoning concept of African Negritude launched in the following decade in the magazine *Black Student* and developed principally by two African writers: Aimé Césaire, then at the École Normale Supérieure, and Léopold Sedar Senghor, the Sorbonne student who was to become President of the Republic of Senegal. African controversy over the term "Negritude" will probably rouse an exploration of its American equivalent, yet to be distinguished, yet to be named. This American Negritude, once defined and compared with "the African personality" and "the black man's identity" as phrases indicative to Césaire and Senghor, will remain traceable in the works of Hughes, its foremost exponent.

If American Negritude can be tentatively defined as that complex of traits, sensibilities, and historical consciousness peculiar to black Americans, a study of Hughes's poetry alone can yield the outline of the concept. The importance of skin color, for example, is revealed in "Negro," "Me and the Mule," "Nightmare Boogie," and "Letter from Spain." His earliest soundings of this theme are serious, respectful. "Negro," which appeared in *The Crisis* in January, 1922, and opened *The Weary Blues*, identifies the Negro's darkness with the night and with "the depths of my Africa"; it gives Negro color specific moral and physical strength. "Dream Variations" manages—besides effects shown in Chapter III—to invest Negro darkness with a fairyland grace and relaxed beauty.

In 1937, Hughes expressed the world-wide implications of this obvious kind of Negritude. His "Letter from Spain/Addressed to Alabama" (the nine-stanza poem quoted in part in Chapter I) opens with "We captured a wounded Moor today./He was just as dark as me." The versified letter shows the quickening bond of color that resolves differences between the dying African and his Negro interrogator.

Two kinds of humor later play upon this theme. "Me and the Mule," in *Shakespeare in Harlem*, gives taut-faced comment on meaningless color:

> I'm like that old mule—
> Black—and don't give a damn!
> You got to take me
> Like I am.

Montage included "Nightmare Boogie," opening with the poet's seeing "a million faces/black as me!" His dream turns nightmare with a quizzical twist, as the faces all are suddenly *"dead white!"* and boogiewoogie music is blaring. A derisive, razzing tone sharpens the anecdotal joviality and hardens the condemnation of color prejudice.

Another component of Negritude is related to skin color but not limited to it: the sense of a particular beauty possessed by Negroes. The earliest-printed poem on the subject is "My People" (in *The Crisis,* June, 1922), a six-line piece which straightforwardly declares the beauty of Negroes' faces, eyes, and souls. But the earliest-written poem on the subject is "When Sue Wears Red" (quoted in Chapter I), in which the sweetness of a brown-faced girl wearing red is made both timeless and regal by references to ancient Egypt and its queens. The author's most sensuously conceived expression of this theme is "Harlem Sweeties" in *Shakespeare in Harlem.* Typical lines flow easily:

> Brown sugar lassie,
> Caramel treat,
> Honey-gold baby
> Sweet enough to eat.
> Peach-skinned girlie,
> Coffee and cream,
> Chocolate darling
> Out of a dream.

The softly bouncing rhythm carries different pulses of adoration: the candy-stocking eagerness of Manhattan whites touring Harlem cabarets, and the Keatsian, rainbow abundance sensed at a Negro beauty pageant.

An important trait encompassed by Negritude is durability, reflected by Dilsey in Faulkner's *The Sound and the Fury,* and emphasized by Hughes all of his life. "Mother to Son," in *The Crisis,* December, 1922, begins the strong matriarchal portraits found in Hughes's poetry and fiction. This poem, using homely images like tacks, splinters, and torn-up boards, shows a poor Negro woman instilling her own persistence into her son. The same unconquerable determination imbues "The Negro Mother," which in 1931 furnished the name for a sequence of Golden Stair Press Broadsides decorated by Prentiss Taylor and marked by Hughes with instructions for dramatic recitation. "The Negro

Mother," which drew a tearful platform embrace from Mary McLeod Bethune when Hughes read it at her college, shows how the speaker's "dream like steel in [her] soul" and her faith in a free tomorrow for her race's children have helped her endure mistreatment and exhort youngsters to "march ever forward, breaking down bars." In the early 1940's, "Spirituals" compares a Negro mother's durability to the firmness of tree roots and mountains; and "Still Here" asserts resistance to all attempts to make the Negro speaker "Stop laughin', stop lovin', stop livin'."

Negro durability is elusive to the understanding as a psychic phenomenon, and Hughes waited till the middle decades of his career as a poet to explore it. Of the two poems in *Fields of Wonder* in which Hughes makes this attempt, "Burden" shows, almost mystically, the psychic pang common to Negroes:

> It is not weariness
> That bows me down,
> But sudden nearness
> To song without sound.

"Oppression" adds brief explication: the dearth of dreams for dreamers, songs for singers—songs that will, however, break their jails. These verses suggest the singing tension of nearness to the rational ideal, so often shattered—in interracial encounters—into empty retrenchment or silent impasse. Clearer, more admonitory lines appear in *Montage*. "Harlem" asks "What happens to a dream deferred?" and gives alternatives: it dries up "like a raisin in the sun," festers, sugars over, sags. *"Or does it explode?"* ends the poem. Remembered partly as the source of Lorraine Hansberry's title for *Raisin in the Sun*, "Harlem" traces in figurative language the long scar of psychic abuse which might, it emphasizes, develop a fatally eruptive itch.

An expression of Negritude important in the 1960's is the recognition of African heritage. Hughes's poems strongly voicing this heritage, however, belong mostly to the early years of his career. About half were written or published in the early 1920's during the ascendancy of Marcus Garvey, whose weekly *Negro World* extolled African history, and whose Black Star Line, Black Madonna, black baby dolls, and revived Back-to-Africa Movement held the attention of much of the world. *The Crisis* published three such poems in eighteen months. "Danse Africaine" (August, 1922) merges deliberate, changing tom-tom beats with wispy whirls of a dancing girl, and the poem is consciously exotic. "Brothers" (February, 1924), with its "Kinsmen—you and I,/You from Africa,/I from the U.S.A.," prosily alphabetizes the heritage. "Lament for Dark Peoples" (June, 1924) plainly pictures red and black men as taken from their primitive homes and "caged in the circus of civilization."

The best poem on this theme is "Our Land" in *The World Tomorrow* (1923). It excels the others in pleasant imagery (twilight is "a soft bandanna handkerchief/Of rose and gold"); but its oversimplification of Negro life—due perhaps to concentration on primitive sources of real value—injures it. "Poem/For the portrait of an African boy after the manner of Gauguin" (printed with "Our Land") and "Afraid" (in *The Weary Blues*) pursue the theme with less beauty of language and without rhyme. Both generalize a Negro fear of civilization: the former poem uses remembered tom-toms and "wild hot moons"; the latter, ancestral cries "among the palms in Africa." The same moon and palm imagery is muted in "Nude Young Dancer," selected by Alain Locke for his *The New Negro* (1925). In this poem a Harlem cabaret and a jungle bower are fused in the fancy of the poet-spectator who senses cleanliness and naturalness in the dancer—a perception consonant with the total meaning of "Harlem Dance Hall" in *Fields of Wonder*.

A farewell to African themes is implicit, even in the title, in "Afro-American Fragment" in *The Crisis* of July, 1930. "So long,/ So far away/Is Africa," it begins, and admits that only history books and African tunes in "strange un-Negro tongue" preserve memories of it. Hughes's later role in perpetuating those memories is foreshadowed:

> Subdued and time-lost
> Are the drums—and yet
> Through some vast mist of race
> There comes this song. . . .

His final approach to Negritude concerns Negroes' historical consciousness of their American past. Its best and its most detailed poetic expressions appear at opposite ends of a thirty-year stretch of creativity. In the chapter of *The Big Sea* named after the first line of "The Negro Speaks of Rivers," Hughes tells how and why, in the summer of 1920, he wrote this perhaps most often anthologized of his poems—one that is a boy's testament of love for his race. Hughes, newly aware of the spiritual strength of migrant Southern Negroes and feeling emotionally cast out by his estranged parents, received melancholy inspiration from the sunset gold upon the Mississippi he was crossing by train. Submerging that feeling into thoughts of mighty rivers in his ancestral past (and having wrestled all day with the problem of hatred of Negroes so vocal in the father who awaited him in Mexico), he reconciled his isolation in a river-like fusion in which history became rebirth, self-justification, and veiled prophecy. The lines first written on the back of an envelope begin the poem thus:

> I've known rivers:
> I've known rivers ancient as the world and older than the flow
> of human blood in human veins.
>
> My soul has grown deep like the rivers.
>
> I bathed in the Euphrates when dawns were young.
> I built my hut near the Congo and it lulled me to sleep.
> I looked upon the Nile and raised the pyramids above it. . . .

The dedication of this poem in *The Weary Blues* to W. E. B. DuBois, and its selection in 1965 by Marian Anderson for inclusion in her farewell concert at Carnegie Hall suggest its comprehensive meaning to Hughes and to the Negro public.

Between 1920 and 1950, the year of publication of the very detailed "Prelude to our Age," several poems employ Negro history. "October 16," in *Opportunity* in 1931, points to Negro participation in John Brown's raid on Harper's Ferry, as does "Freedom's Plow." Sometimes a single line appealing to Negro historical consciousness transforms a poem. The use of "John Henry with his hammer" inflames the imagery of sparks and sundering crucial to "Love" in *Shakespeare in Harlem*. And just before "Prelude to Our Age," Hughes circles back to his obliquely autobiographical interest: "Shame on You" (in *Phylon*, Spring, 1950) criticizes Harlemites for not naming a building after John Brown. Dwarfing previous poems in its very purpose, "Prelude to Our Age" (in *Branch Library Book News* of the New York Public Library for October, 1950) mentions over sixty persons known in Negro history, and related organizations and events.

Negritude, then, referring to Negroes' various traits and sensibilities, and emphasizing their feelings about their beauty, durability, and history, defines itself in Hughes's works with as much clarity as the national mind brings to the concept. Basic details, stark outlines, nuances—all are revealed. They amass and enliven a tradition as much literary as sociological in its implications. And a final aspect of Negro soul is widely perceived, though seldom fully comprehended: humor. According to Hughes's Introduction to *The Best of Negro Humor* (1945), even Negroes, especially writers and publishers, often undervalue its uses. Hughes's own uses of humor, ample in his personal conversation and in much of his work, can be only minimally surveyed in this approach to it in the light that it throws on Negroes.

The combined uniqueness and utility of Negro humor has long been its power to conceal and transform, the uniqueness deriving from the magnitude and the persistence of the concealment. The common theme of the mask, then, has an uncommon significance as expression of Negro soul. Hughes labored early to express his sense of the tightness of the mask. When "Minstrel Man" appeared in *The Crisis* (December, 1925), a companion poem, "The Jester," appeared in *Opportunity*. Only "Minstrel Man," discussed in Chapter II, does justice to the theme. The other poem is too plain an exhortation.

Much later, two poems in *One-Way Ticket*, "Life Is Fine" and "Juice Joint: Northern City," show how the author's more elastic humor moderates the grimness of the mask. In the former poem, the mask (a shivering protestation that *"Life is fine!/Fine as wine!"*) is clapped on by the speaker after his discovery that suicide in a cold river or from a high window is strenuous. Here the mask is fitted out of nonracial circumstances; but the expression itself, mixing blues and boogiewoogie style and italicized racial accent, is Negro. "Juice Joint" uses the interruption of a blues song by a sudden dance step, "to keep the gall from biting in [the singer's] mouth," to show the snapping on of the mask. After the adjustment, the Negro women (using gestures precisely like those of the singer Pearl Bailey) "switch their skirts and lift their straightened heads/To sing about the men who've done them wrong."

Not until the 1940's did Hughes begin to publish a number of simply amusing or funny poems. They show a vascular part in the tissue of Negro experience. Their humor differs from that occasionally found in the blues poems—such as in "Wide River" of *The Dream Keeper*—in that it belongs less to a tradition than to the literary being of the author. In "Bed Time" (in *Shakespeare in Harlem*) the amusing blink of the speaker is more of a departure for Hughes than it seems. Having retired in the too-quiet house after the exit of his woman, he reflects: "Listen at them mice./Do I see a couple? Or did I count twice?" In a two-line poem in the same volume, "Little Lyric (Of Great Importance)," the speaker's upturned eyes and caustic "I wish the rent/Was heaven sent" are part of a continual grimace in Harlem; and Hughes had not forgotten the triple rent charged Negroes in the Cleveland of his youth. "If-ing," in the same book, is pure waggishness. *One-Way Ticket's* humorous "Jitney" remarkably captures, in its linear form and bumpy dialogue, a cab ride up and down Chicago's South Parkway. "Bad Morning" is a tattered little portrait of the absurdly undefeated lowly:

> Here I sit
> With my shoes mismated.
> Lawdy-mercy!
> I's frustrated!

The poet's humor finds, in the subject of death, a means of disclosing the toughness and resiliency of Negro soul. One of his earliest poems in this vein is "Wake," in *Shakespeare in Harlem:*

> Tell all my mourners
> To mourn in red—
> Cause there ain't no sense
> In my bein' dead.

This poem, reflecting the folk spirit of Harlem as well as ritual visible to Hughes in 1930 in Haiti, was followed the next year by "Too Blue," printed in *Contemporary Poetry*. In this poem the speaker's melancholy masks his strength in rejecting suicide —on the argument that his hard head would require two bullets. "Deceased," in *One-Way Ticket*, uses an anecdote about death ("The licker/Was lye"); and in "Hope," in *Montage*, a Harlem wife converts her husband's dying request for fish into a hopeful numbers bet. The latter poem scores the obsessiveness that both creates and destroys exploitation of human miseries.

Some of Hughes's humor plays upon varieties of distortion akin to that in "Hope." In "Could Be" (in *One-Way Ticket*) the lines "When you pawned my watch/You pawned my heart" and

"Any place is dreary/Without my watch and you" show how humorous expression in personal relations can gauge the twisting of responses under economic or other duress. In "Necessity" (in *Montage*) the author exposes the folk jibe, "I don't have to do nothing/but eat, drink, stay black, and die," to an amoral correction: Negroes must work hard—to survive rental overcharges. The obscure web of oppression, defense, and consequent ambiguity of some expressions of the Negro soul indicates the complexity of life examined by Hughes.

Unique is the humorous "Madam to You" series of poems, first so named and grouped in *One-Way Ticket*. Separately they had begun to appear in *Poetry* (September, 1943) and in *Common Ground* (Winter, 1943). Subtitled "The Life and Times of Alberta K. Johnson," the twenty-five-page series emphasizes the business, domestic, and personal life of the protagonist. She is Hughes's Negro matriarch turned small entrepreneur, his folk-minded lover turned middle-aged divorcee making her way among rent gougers and number writers. He merges style and content entertainingly in the dramatic monologue "Madam and the Phone Bill," in which Alberta K. refuses to pay for a call she took from a boy friend in Kansas City. Her character and her plight are deepened in "Madam and Her Might-Have-Been": after having two husbands, she rather soured her life through lack of trust. Hard times have scratched into her memory that

> When you think you got bread
> It's always a stone—
> Nobody loves nobody
> For yourself alone.

The humor that enlivened the author's fiction at the start and increasingly marked his poetry of the 1940's settled deepest in his prose. One night in 1942 in a Harlem gin mill near his St. Nicholas Avenue address, Hughes received the most authentic comic inspiration of his life. He overheard the man who was to become his own fictional Jesse B. Semple explaining to a girl friend his job of making cranks in a New Jersey war plant. In reply to Hughes's question as to what the cranks cranked the Negro worker shrugged: "I don't know what them cranks cranks. You know white folks don't tell Negroes what cranks cranks." His notion of a separate white world, his engagingly fresh diction while objecting to it, became a study of the author during their many later bar-stool conversations.

While Hughes took Boswellian notes after the conversations, a literary character was being born who represented the flesh and spirit of Harlem, a folk hero sprung of the common black man. He was a whole personality when Hughes found himself arguing with him at the typewriter while the worker was miles away. His vivid reality on paper now had the dimensions that would earn him full comparison to Huck Finn, Mr. Dooley, and Uncle Remus.[12] When the original of Simple—as he came to be called—moved out of the author's life to the Bronx in 1950 with a bandaged head, Hughes had distilled his attitudes in over a hundred and fifty weekly *Chicago Defender* columns, and *Simple Speaks His Mind* was about to be published. *Simple Takes a Wife* (1953), *Simple Stakes a Claim* (1957), and *Simple's Uncle Sam* (1965) would follow.

Negro soul is steadily revealed by this folk character who has been called the Negro Everyman. Simple is fully savored only by listening to him talk of his pending divorce from Isabel in Baltimore; his delights and dilemmas in courting the refined Joyce in Harlem; and his opinions on numerous subjects ranging from suspicious landladies to chocolate lingerie, from eating pork chops at the front window to playing "the white folks' dozens," from atom bombs to cellophane bandannas. Leaning on a bar or a mailbox, Simple unburdens himself with the robust wit and common sense everywhere typical of an alert man of the people.

The energetic jazz idiom marks Simple's speech and bursts of doggerel; the verses on the house-rent party cards which so attract him ("Hop, Mister Bunny,/Skip, Mister Bear!/If you don't dig this party/You ain't nowhere") show the appeal of lively diction to the Negro community—and Hughes himself retains many such cards from the 1930's. The lyrical expression of this strand of Negroes' lives is delightfully recorded in the author's musical folk comedy, *Simply Heavenly*.

Among facets of Negritude seen in Hughes's poems, attitudes toward skin color appear in every Simple book. Of his grandfather, Simple proudly says that "he were black." He feels that because a lecturing historian—"hysterian" to Simple—is "black as me" he should not castigate Negroes so severely for their faults. In the second Simple book a whole chapter is devoted to

"That Word Black." The protagonist's sense of Negro beauty is evident in his ravishment by all shades of feminine charm. The durability of the race is stressed in Hughes's everpresent still-here theme in the chapter "Final Fear" of the first volume, in which Simple declares: "I have been fired, laid off, . . . Jim Crowed, segregated, barred out, insulted, eliminated, called black, yellow, and red, locked in, locked out, locked up, also left holding the bag. I have been caught in the rain, caught in raids, caught short with my rent, and caught with another man's wife. . . but I am still here!" "If Negroes can survive white folks in Mississippi," Simple says in his third book, "we can survive anything" —meaning the atom bomb.

Psychic oppression is pointed out by Simple in his comments on wartime V-bombs: "To be shot down is bad for the body, but to be Jim Crowed is worse for the spirit." In *Simple Takes a Wife,* he explains about policemen who speak abusively to him merely because he walks through a white neighborhood: "If they do not hit me, they have already hurt my soul." He tells why he recommended a Negro university (Lincoln, Hughes's alma mater) to Franklin D. Roosevelt Brown, his second cousin: racial snubs in a white school "would hurt that boy to his heart."

African heritage is emphasized only in the first chapter of the first Simple book, as the Harlemite speaks of his great-great grandfather: "He must of been simple—else why did he let them capture him in Africa and sell him for a slave to breed my great-grandpa in slavery to breed my grandpa in slavery to breed my pa to breed me to look at that window [in the 1943 riots] and say, 'It ain't mine! Bam-mmm-mm-m!' and kick it out?" In a later chapter, "Ways and Means," a related aspect of Negritude, the historical consciousness of Negro experience in America, explains Simple's rationalization of his participation in the riot: ". . . let them white men spend some of the profits they make out of Harlem . . . out of these high rents in Harlem all these years to put them windows back. Also let 'em use some of that money . . . they owe my grandmother and my great-grandmother and her mother before that for working all them years in slavery for nothing. . . ."

This consciousness reappears in the second book when Simple says Negroes should be memorialized on stamps. Like the speaker in "Daybreak in Alabama," Simple sees himself composing a humanitarian song. But his would recapture the story of the black Wise Man, achieving a union important in Hughes's fiction and poetry: an identification with historical divinity. "It would be *my* song . . . like as if I was there myself . . . and *I* seen the star. . . . And when I riz up from bending over that Baby in the Manager I were strong and not afraid," Simple explains.

The third book pursues this stratum in two ways. Simple's new wife talks about the "black Greeks," Cleopatra "of the colored race," and the biblical Sheba of King Solomon, "black but comely." Turning to style rather than content, Hughes purveys historical consciousness with hot barbs of wit mixed with jabbing satire. His picture of brutalities in Mississippi in the chapter "Simple Stashes Back" is both Swiftian and rib-tickling. In "Four-Way Celebrations" Simple's ideas about a White History Week to celebrate long exploitation of Negroes are trenchant. His suggestions about a Sisterhood Week for the Protection of White Womanhood, devoted to the realistic commemoration of lynchings, is reminiscent of the great English satirist's *Modest Proposal*.

Humorous style in these books is not easily separable from content. Close study of them reveals about a score of distinguishable topics humorously illuminated by Simple's talk, and about the same number of separate styles of humor. The equal marriage of content and style in the humor is shown by the fact that about half of these styles are funny because of the comical light thrown over the topic by the rapid, versatile play of Simple's folk mind. The author's most typical subjects—all broadly classifiable somewhere under racial life—are Simple's character-revealing background and present attitudes and imaginings, his race-consciousness, and intermarriage. His most typical styles of humor are derived from verbal play, long lists, comical ways of stating the miscellaneous truths of discrimination, and tall-tale exuberance.

A deeper analysis of the Simple books should be made. It is worthwhile sociologically to synthesize Simple's comments on American delusions, white liberals, foreigners, Negro leaders, and the South. It is profitable esthetically to comprehend how ingeniously he extracts humor from absolutely odd notions, expressed and implied etymologies, turnabouts, and the illusoriness of race itself. These effects and topics are also found in short stories imbedded in the Simple books, especially in "A Dog Named Trilby" and in "A Veteran Falls," the best ones.[13] Special subtleties merit examination: how Simple bewilders a white employer and later outwits his "colleged" friend Boyd by assuming in both instances that he is white; how his ten or more flights of fancy deeply reveal his true nature; and how his sermon imagined for his own funeral ("Oh, precious soul of Jesse B., worth more than words can tell!"), though edged in nonsense, is one of the seals of his humanity.

The Simple books as repositories of both Negro soul and the author's wit can be suggested by a few passages. His Negro Everyman uses many phrases common to folk Negroes, such as "low-rate," "pull a teck," "sure is a blip"; and a chapter in the first book opens, "What's on the rail for the lizard . . . ?" Half of "Night in Harlem" in the second book exhibits the verbal play folk imaginations enjoy as Simple logically mixes titles of "colored" movies into his defense before a judge: "*Pinky* was light, but not right. That boy in *Lost Boundaries* was near white, but things was tight. In *Home of the Brave* all we could do was rave—there were *No Way Out*. Couldn't even jump in *The Well* —because it were hell! So, I ask you, Your Honery, what's it all about?"

In "Tickets and Takers" in the same book, Simple is witty in verbal dalliance at a bar with a girl who is his match. He opens:

> "Waiting for me?"
> "Only till my 100 Proof comes along."
> "Baby, cannot you tell I am bottled in bond, also aged in wood?"
> "You do look aged. But . . . I love settled men."

Simple having braved her warning about Joe, they continue:

> "Joe is a man who does not take no tea for the fever," she stated. "If I wasn't a woman, I would be scared of Joe myself."
> "Most womens *would* put their head in a lion's mouth," said Simple. "But as pretty as your head is, wouldn't no lion bite it off. But some man might knock it off."
> "Joe aims the other way. . . . When he gets through, there is *him* and *me* standing there. But *you* are on the ground."

Humorous compilations, like one near the start of the first book, sometimes evoke images especially meaningful to Negroes: "These feet have supported everything from a cotton bale to a hongry woman. These feet have walked ten thousand miles working for white folks and another ten thousand keeping up with colored. These feet have stood at altars, crap tables, free lunches, bars, graves, kitchen doors, betting windows, hospital clinics, WPA desks, social security railings, and in all kinds of lines from soup lines to the draft." In the second volume, with his mouth watering for a pot of greens, Simple lists thirteen different kinds from his store of "greenology."

He expresses truisms of democracy with force and humor. In "Something to Lean On" in the first volume, he complains that when a Negro tries to lean on the Constitution, it falls down on him. He adds: "But Southerners can beat you, burn you, lynch you, and hang you to a tree—and every one of them will go scotfree. . . . I can lean on this bar, but I ain't got another thing in the U.S.A. on which to lean." The line from this injustice to his blackness is straight, and Simple spells out his sense of the permanence of both, in the previous chapter: "I am a Son of Ham from down in 'Bam—and there ain't none other like I am. Solid black from front to back! And one thing sure—it won't fade, jack!"

The exaggeration of the tall tale, often heard in the animated exchanges in Negro barber shops and lounging places, seems a natural endowment of Simple's. "Baltimore Womens" in *Simple Takes a Wife* gains vividly from his recollections of bedbugs, big and defiant enough to speak churlishly to hotel transients, lap up kerosene as if it were refreshment, and parachute down from the ceiling. In the same book, Simple tells of Jimboy, whose new white wife soured the glances of Joyce and her friends at a dance. The blonde went home alone to Arkansas to bear her child near her liberal family. Almost three months overdue, the "brownskin baby was singing real loud" when the white doctor pressed his stethoscope to the mother's stomach, protesting that he would not be born in the South: "As long as South is South,/I won't come out!"

Jesse B. Semple, whose name satirizes whites who "know"—and know how to handle—his kind, is unforgettable. He is objective, as when he expands to a global view of the color problem; and he is subjective, as when he stubbornly defends his bad grammar and his race-consciousness. He has a prophetic intuition of the unbalance in whites who cling to a faltering rack of privileges. Just once he loses his sense of humor, in "Mississippi Fists" in the third book, speaking of Emmett Till: "I can feel them fists in MY own face right now, and them white men's kicks here in the middle of ME right now, and their big old, hairy old hands around MY throat so I cannot cry out loud, and that rope tied onto ME with that heavy old iron wheel from the cotton gin pulling ME down in that muddy old, dirty old, stinking, sluggish old river. . . ."

Simple comes in strong doses, his strength relaxed in comic readiness as earthy as his suggestions for Negro magazine covers: " 'Can Sex Pass?' would be my *first* article. . . . In the second issue, I would have on the cover in big letters, 'Sex Seized in Passing.' In the third issue I would have, 'Please Pass the Sex' in red headlines."

After the third Simple book, a minimum of a hundred and twenty-nine reviews were available in periodicals and newspapers, forty-one of them foreign; and Hughes soon accumulated thirty or so personal letters of commentary. Reviewers placed the contents of the books in twenty-one different categories, ranging from snippet to tale to novel. The various judgments boil down around the truth of the book jacket phrases. Jesse B. Semple is indeed "a major figure in American literature." For every Negro, there is much in him to love. For every American, there is much in him to learn.

Humor in Negro experience, as expressed in Hughes's short fiction outside the stories mingled in the Simple books, shapes the material in about ten narratives. Some are mere sketches: "Name in the Papers" and "Heaven to Hell" are lively but slight. "Pushcart Man" is a picturesque vignette of Harlem moving the reader behind a shouting vendor's cart of "pomatoes and totatoes," past the language of arguments, abortive fights, and an old man's metaphor roused by a fat woman in slacks.

Three stories written in three different decades adequately represent fictional humor not already mentioned. "Slice Him Down" was drafted in Reno in 1933 (the author revealed in talking of it in September, 1960) and was first published, with vivid illustrations, in *Esquire* in May, 1936. It highlights the mock-razor duel of Terry and Sling, Negro vagabonds who took the garbage-can and freight-train route to segregated Reno. Hughes extracts rough humor from an alley-bound environment of poverty and discrimination. The extra vest, lemon-cream shirt, grey sweatshirt, and ragged purple sweater that save Sling from a razor thrust are Hughes's grim but willing compromise with the *Esquire* editor who wanted the original tragic ending changed. The garments worn one over another are a black hobo's defense against winter.

The common Negroes of "Slice Him Down," pressed into a Reno alley, fashion their humor outside the glamor of the sign many of them were not allowed to learn how to read, "The BIGGEST little CITY in the WORLD." Terry's Angelina angers Sling's Charlie-Mae with remarks about riffraff and "womens what don't know they name" and is repaid by a slap sped from the folds of a rabbit-skin coat, accompanied by the epithet, "old stuck-up yellow hussy." Spectators of the hoboes' fight climb on stools, tables, and beer kegs; and at the piano seems to sit the protagonist of the ten-year-old "The Weary Blues": "a little, fat, coal-black man in shirt sleeves with a glass of gin by his side." The author-narrator uses caricature, making Terry's face "a shiny oval under his derby." And the vagabonds' Saturday night clothing, mixing sky-blue, honey-brown, and the swinging gold of key chains, adds comical garishness.

An epistolary story written the same autumn, "Passing," deals with a phenomenon tragic and humorous; but the humor of it did not show in Hughes's fiction until 1941. Then at Hollow Hills Farm he wrote another story of the same name, derived "almost exactly," he said in conversation, from an experience shared with "Aaron Douglas[14] . . . and two or three other writers of the 1920's." Published as "Who's Passing for Who?" in 1945 (in *Negro Story* for December-January), the story recalls the Harlem Renascence night that an interracial group had some confused fun brawling, meandering, and ultimately guessing one another's racial identities.

The humor is satirically aimed at the pretensions of the Harlem literati and their white friends. Redheaded Iowan Stubblefield fights for a blonde struck by a Negro, only to find that she is the man's Negro wife. The other Iowans, Negroes by their own gradual confession, declare at the end from their cab: "We're white. We just thought we'd kid you by passing for colored. . . ." The Negro writers are appropriately left at the curb; throughout the story, they have remained superciliously on the edge of the Harlem stage that caught the imagination of white Manhattan and faraway Negro artists. The writers snub everyone not privy to the mysteries of Gertrude Stein, Man Ray, and Jean Toomer; they ignore the works of the previous generation, even James Weldon Johnson's; they, too, are passing, and they know it well. But Negro soul, as visible in the facts, anecdotes, and subtleties of passing, is not revealed to any depth inaccessible to overt wit. Closely reading "Passing" in *The Ways of White Folks,* one sees much irony and anguish in this old American custom.

Hughes finds comedy on Harlem's sophisticated Sugar Hill. "Patron of the Arts," written not long before the spring of 1951[15] but first published in *The Langston Hughes Reader,* tells the end of a love affair between a young Oklahoma artist and a green-eyed Harlem charmer over twice his age. In a typical scene, Darby reminds Cornelia that her husband might interrupt them with firearms. "Let him," she cries. "First we'll mix a cocktail." Darby abstains. Seeing him speedily donning his coat, she threatens suicide; but she pours a drink for herself instead. The humor is "smart" (with embarrassed pose, bright dialogue, and tables turned); however, the story reveals little that is distinctive of Negro spirit.

But the story has the most beautiful humanizing touch in Hughes's fiction. Cornelia's final small note, asking Darby to take his painting of her back to Oklahoma "to remember how your patron looked," transforms her. Without it, she would have been just another aging woman trying, with cosmetics, wardrobe, cash, and someone else's inexperience and need, to soften the hand of time. With it, she seems thoughtful and sensitive, wishing for her young man—no doubt in vain—a return to the innocence of his drawing board. She wants him to remember her in his maturity, not as an older woman who lied about her age to be with him, but as Mrs. Oldham, his patron, who had some respect for art.

The works discussed in this chapter suggest the magnitude of the young Hughes's vision of his task as a writer; they indicate the versatility of his spiral approaches to the Negro soul. Life and love, inside and outside the veil of color, become subjects as wide as the author's sympathies, yet as specific as artistic integrity alone can make them. In every division and subdivision of topic that marks the boundaries chosen, the author has produced work worthy of either admiration or respectful study.

CHAPTER *6*

A Wheel in Harlem

I could take the Harlem night
and wrap around you,
Take the neon lights and make a crown . . .
        —"Juke Box Love Song"

OVER HALFWAY through the 1960's, Hughes still pivots in his swivel-chair near the center of Harlem, turning to share his busy life with a visitor or to open the file cabinet behind his desk. The weight of years has touched his frame and hairline without apparently diminishing his energy of movement or the liveliness of his light brown features. Occasionally brushing from his chest a long ash from a cigarette, he speaks rapidly and so fluidly that one sometimes misses a word. His easy gestures indicate a histrionic flair, and his alert eyes are attentive but not restive. Less than average in height, he moves actively in his third-floor studio lined with books international in variety, each room slowly narrowing as the many hundreds of books, African curios, and record albums vie for space with manuscripts, letters, clippings, plaques, and filing cases. Bespectacled and genial at his typewriter, fingering a pencilled telephone number on his "bulletin board" above the desk, or hospitably mixing a gin and tonic, Hughes remains a genuine cosmopolite.

The author's time-consuming correspondence and theatrical involvements have decreased his poetic efforts, but he has produced new works during the 1960's. Some have been inspired by individual occasions. "And So the Seed" was written for a testimonial dinner honoring the Jelliffes of Karamu House in 1963. The Harlem riot of the next year evoked his caustic "Harlem Call" (*American Dialog,* October-November, 1964). The tender "Silent One" (*The New York Times,* November 9, 1962) represents the continuation of his nonracial lyrical strain. "Doorknobs" (*The Outsider,* No. 1, 1961), beginning "The simple silly terror/ of a doorknob on a door," shows the restless yawing of contemporary rhythm and meaning so evident in his *Ask Your Mama* (1961). In *The Panther and the Lash* (1967), Hughes offers some of his poems, both old and new, that reflect the racially turbulent years climaxed by the Black Panther Party and the "white backlash." Besides seasonal greetings to friends, his miscellaneous poetry of the 1960's includes satisfying brief pieces like "The Innocent" and the almost mystical "Small Memory," as well as "Journey into Space," subtitled "A Musical Adventure for Baritone, Trumpet, and Drums."

Reading poems to music remains the poet's specialty. Negro spirituals worked by George Bass into narrative form accompanied his reading at Rutgers University in 1961. A Langston Hughes Issue of his alma mater's *The Lincoln University Bulletin*, in 1964, commemorated his visit there by printing his readings, such as "Hold Fast to Dreams." Records, radio, and television have also multiplied his audience. The 1964 Emmy Award-winning television show, "Beyond the Blues," used at least six of his poems, including "The Negro Speaks of Rivers," "Mother to Son," "Negro Dancers," and "When Sue Wears Red." Writing a 1965 Easter script for the same network, CBS, Hughes worked into "It's a Mighty World" (sung by Odetta strolling on the California coast) a few poems from *Fields of Wonder*. With D. G. Bridson of the British Broadcasting Company, he prepared "The Negro in America" series, which late in 1964 used some of his work in "Negro Poetry Today," readings by poets he introduced.

Composers and publishers of music continue their long interest in Hughes's poetry. During the 1960's, Margaret Bonds, who often collaborated with him, has made use of his poems. Her "Songs of the Seasons," a cycle based on pieces in *Fields of Wonder* and first played in Chicago in 1960, has been part of later tributes to Hughes in New York: at the Brooklyn Museum, for example, where he received an award from the National Association of Negro Musicians in 1963, and where he was accorded special birthday honors in 1964.

I Ask Your Mama

Hughes's most sustained long poetic work is *Ask Your Mama*. Subtitled "12 Moods for Jazz," it prints the melody of "Hesitation Blues" as its leitmotif, has marginal notes for musical accompaniment, and appends "Liner Notes for the Poetically

Unhep." Visually striking, its color format reflects the author's admiration for Duke Ellington, whose *Black, Brown and Beige* matches the poet's twelve moods and explains the alternating blue and brown ink on beige paper—called terracotta, salmon- and pumpkin-colored by various reviewers.

The unusual appearance of *Ask Your Mama*, with its cubistic six-color binding, suits its unusual content, which both attracted and bemused many readers. Reviewers used terms like "avant- garde," "semi-revolutionary" (*Virginia Kirkus Bulletin*), and "patchwork" (*Library Journal*) to suggest its style. They noted its thematic unity—emphasized by the refrain "in the quarter of the Negroes"—and its rhythmical suitability to the jazz, blues, and drums in the intended background. But they saw limitations as well as merits in its topical allusions and in its proposed musical accompaniment. Among academic critics, Rudi Blesh and Saunders Redding, in reviews in the *New York Herald Tribune* and the *Baltimore Afro-American* respectively, praised Hughes's updating a tradition of his own creation in the 1920's.

The principal effects of *Ask Your Mama* require no musical background. Although lines like "Boundaries bind unbinding" add only percussion, and others like "Ina-Youra at the masthead" mean almost nothing to readers unacquainted with the names of the Qualls family, Hughes's "range of subtle nuances is new," as mentioned, though not detailed, by Redding. His references to Negro history and racial oppression are often pointed. It is his still unanalyzed style that is subtle.

Concerning that style, the title itself—the crucial phrase in "playing the dozens," a mildly insulting folk-Negro game of invective against the participants' ancestry—is employed in the poem as innuendo hinting at the nation's unacknowledged inter- racial family trees. Sometimes Hughes plays with a phrase as if it were a ball to dribble:

> In the quarter of the Negroes
> Where Negroes sing so well
> Negroes sing so well
> Sing so well
> So well.
> Well?

Sometimes he uses literary counterpoint. At the end of "Gospel Cha-Cha," he juxtaposes lines of religious and secular names with lines narrating the climb to Calvary. Finding among the three on that hill that "one, yes, one/was black as me," the speaker immediately ends the section with "Cha-cha . . . cha-cha/Cha." This indifferent turnabout, contrasting in mood and meaning with an esthetic experiment which it terminates, compares to other poems like "Dream Boogie."

At times accumulated meaning takes other turns. Hughes can spurt compact allusions in single lines, such as "Alioune Aimé Sedar sips his Negritude" (capitalized, like all words in the poem). This line fuses the given names of three founders of the concept of Negritude: Diop, Césaire, and Senghor. "Bird in Orbit" has a passage as economical:

> That gentleman in expensive shoes
> Made from the hides of blacks
> Who tips among the shadows
> Soaking up the music
> Asked me right at Christmas
> Did I want to eat with white folks?

These lines merge the themes of economic, sexual, and cultural exploitation rather humorously in a person made more out of place than ever by his boldness and poor timing in asking a naïve personal question.

A certain fluidity of time and illusiveness of place hover over the poem. The evocation of the distant African past in the third stanza of the book is embodied suddenly, in the fourth stanza, in an African diplomat of 1961, "sent by the State Department/ . . . to meet the blacks." Later, a vicious bloodhound that "tears the body from the shadow" becomes as faint as the shadow itself —unreal in the sudden, pertinent context of filibuster, thunder, and Four Roses. In "Blues in Stereo," references to Stanleyville and long-playing records blend continents, and the lines "Where an ancient river flows/Past huts that house a million blacks" use the river image to dissolve time and space.

Extra unity derives from both obvious and subtle means. A child's vainly repeated request for show fare (reflecting at once a Southern idiom asking for fair play) carries the hard-times theme from the fourth section until the final lines, "Show fare, Mama./Show fare!" Lines in the early and the final pages denote the unifying undercurrent guiding the poet: the "Shades of Pigmeat" section, exploring modes of oppression, declares, "Answer questions answer/And answers with a question," a truth echoed near the end of the book in the conclusion that "the tell me of the mama/Is the answer to the child."

Also indirect are the symbolic uses of Niagara Falls and the mythical unicorn. Apart from the significance of the former to rescued slaves nearing Canada, explained in "Liner Notes," several references to frozen Niagara and to "Niagara of the Indians!/Niagara of the Congo!" emerge as images of freedom congealed, of dreams deferred. Thus "Original Niagara N.A.A.C.P." alludes both to the Niagara Movement of 1905-1909 as forerunner of the National Association for the Advancement of Colored People and to the meanings of freedom related to the latter organization. The poet uses the second figure to suggest brotherhood among dark nations as a feeling "untaken down on tape" by folklorists, that it may be on safari, "Where game to bag's illusive/As a silver unicorn." The creature defines the quest of black students at the Sorbonne: "But why ride on mule or donkey/When there's a unicorn?" Closer to Harlem, Martin Luther King "mounts his unicorn/Oblivious to blood/And moonlight on its horn." Like Niagara Falls, the mythical figure means dynamic freedom. Both symbols are phenomena beyond corruption.

Hughes, mixing the comfortable rhythm of *Hiawatha* and the quirky modes of the 1960's with his feeling for the vibrant within the slang and the pose, turns these "12 Moods for Jazz" into an oddly balanced work of old and new tensions. Beautifully developing phrases are aborted in satirical ones; "lovely lieder" and "collard greens" vie for sensory appeal; commercial signs and advertising cant rise next to fresh imagery. But it all fits in a jangling world of disparate customs and languages. Hughes characteristically mixes his moods and his main interest in the plight of the urban Negro:

> Down the long hard row that I been hoeing
> I thought I heard the horn of plenty blowing.
> But I got to get a new antenna, Lord—
> My TV keeps on snowing.

II   *The Gospel Song-Plays*

Two kinds of musical productions occupied Hughes in 1960. His one-act opera, *Port Town*, with music by Jan Meyerowitz, was performed in August at the Boston Symphony's summer center at Tanglewood in Lenox, Massachusetts. More representative of his new theatrical efforts was *Ballad of the Brown King*, a Christmas cantata presenting the story of the titular king among the Three Wise Men. With music by Margaret Bonds, the cantata, dedicated to Martin Luther King, was performed December 11 at the Clark Auditorium of the New York YMCA.

Exactly one year later, Hughes's most successful elaboration of the same story appeared at New York's 41st Street Theater. *Black Nativity* (conceived as "Wasn't That a Mighty Day"), with an all-Negro cast, dramatizes the Christmas story in dialogue, narrative, pantomime, gospel song, folk spirituals, and dance. Embracing for Negroes, in their own music and folk idiom and imagery, the story so many peoples have adapted, Hughes established the dimensions of the "gospel song-play" and gave it an international reputation. By emphasizing the singing of the gospel stars Marion Williams, Alex Bradford, and Princess Stewart, *Black Nativity* moved through the York Playhouse and President Kennedy's International Jazz Festival to the Festival of Two Worlds at Spoleto, Italy, in 1962.

A *New York Times* correspondent reported from Spoleto on July 22: "Sophisticated Italian audiences . . . greeted 'Black Nativity' with enthusiasm, taking part in the singing and hand-clapping and insisting on curtain call after curtain call. . . . The staid Rome newspaper *Il Tempo* wrote that . . . 'The elegant festival public appeared to have forgotten itself, lost in this rhythmic wave that overwhelmed it, an integral part itself of a spectacle that bound stage and auditorium in a [mystical] fusion.'" In London and elsewhere in England, and in Oslo, Brussels, Copenhagen, Hamburg, and Rotterdam, *Black Nativity* triumphed before its return to New York for Christmas season performances at the new Lincoln Center. More Continental and American tours in 1963 and 1964, more performances abroad in 1965, and speculations that it might become an annual Christmas program in New York indicate its irresistibility.

In the early 1960's Hughes produced several other gospel song-plays, but none achieved comparable success. *Gospel Glow*, performed a few times in Brooklyn in October, 1962, and described in the author's program notes as the "first Negro passion play, depicting the Life of Christ, from the cradle to the cross," attracted small notice. In November, 1963, *Tambourines to Glory* had twenty-five performances in the newly renovated Little Theater. Evolving from some of his poems turned into gospel songs by Jobe Huntley in 1953, through his play written around the songs in 1956 and his novel *Tambourines to Glory* of 1958, the play received a little less praise than blame in the New York press. Comments in *The New Yorker*, the *Times*, and the *Herald Tribune* typically censured the poor balance between predictable, sometimes melodramatic narrative and jubilant song. This play, which originated in Hughes's reflections on Harlem's many storefront churches,[1] profits from the talents of Clara Ward, Hilda Simms, and Louis Gosset; but the humor and vigor in its portrait of the occasional bad seed in Harlem's thickly planted ministry shine more steadily in the novel.

Within two months after the closing of *Tambourines, Jerico-Jim Crow* opened in Greenwich Village. Employing spirituals, gospel songs, freedom songs, and two lyrics by Hughes himself, this play achieves unity by weaving its music around the narrative of the Negroes' long struggle for freedom. The history is often gripping, is usually instinct with some optimism, even humor. The musical mood was rousing when the Hugh Porter Gospel Singers marched through the aisles to the improvised stage, strongly moving when young Gilbert Price sang Hughes's prophetic "Freedom Land," and sentimental when Rosalie King and Hilda Harris rendered "Such a Little King." Joseph Attles, who played Chicken-Crow-for-Day in *Tambourines,* was a versatile instrument for picturesque humor. The play ran from January through April.

In May, *The Prodigal Son* made the Greenwich Mews Theater resound to booming song and hand clapping and foot stomping as the forces of sin and virtue took sides in acting the biblical parable. Paired with Bertolt Brecht's *The Exception and the Rule,* Hughes's play seemed, by contrast, all swinging vitality and joy. Using little dialogue, it shaped the devil in the exciting form of Glory Van Scott as Jezebel. Her blandishments overpowered singer and dancer Philip A. Stamps until the gospel-wielding mother (Jeanette Hodge), chief Exhorter (Joseph Attles), and Sister Lord (Dorothy Drake of *Jerico-Jim Crow*) triumphed for virtue. This one-act play, which also contains lyrics by Hughes, has somewhat less value than *Jerico,* but it is lively entertainment. It played till fall before its tour abroad.

III *Prose for a Changing World*

Fittingly in 1960, when seventeen African nations became independent, Hughes published *The First Book of Africa*. Written with a simple grace and power attractive to the young, it outlines the exploration and colonization of Africa. It shows the individual and tribal differences reflected in Africa's historical glories and present crises. The presence of over forty political units and of over seven hundred languages and dialects and the combination of color discrimination and exploitative greed are examples of challenges Hughes shows facing emergent Africa.

Two years later, he brought out *Fight for Freedom: The Story of the NAACP*. Describing the organization at the outset as the most famous, most talked-about, most written-about and most damned and praised group of respectable citizens in America, he traces its fifty years as "the world's biggest law firm." The story and photographs—factual and dramatic, horrifying and heartening—weave biographical sketches of both great and relatively unknown crusaders into a historical narrative. Helping again to keep the record straight, this book records the NAACP's role in Negro America's slow emergence into freedom.

IV *The Editor, Harlem, U.S.A.*

Seven years before *The First Book of Africa,* Hughes's editorial senses had been stirred upon his judging many short stories by South Africans, entries in a contest sponsored by the Johannesburg magazine *Drum*. Taken at first by the notion of editing stories for teenagers,[2] Hughes decided to request material from all over Africa. The result was *An African Treasury* (1960), a compilation of essays, speeches, folk tales, stories, and poems by black Africans, the first truly indigenous group expression of its kind to be printed. The editor's introduction announces the unifying idea, the concept of the African personality, and points out its illustration in various selections. Reviews in both America and Africa—that by Ulli Beier in Lagos's *Daily Express*, for example—recognize how the volume coheres around the concept. From Ghanaian essays on poetic techniques (and whale funerals) to vigorous South African pieces on "pigmentocracy" and Alabama-style racial etiquette, the book shows a style of life and letters of substantial interest.

When Hughes's increasing editorial labors were again published, in 1963, a minor emphasis in *An African Treasury* (seen as a defect in poet Ezekiel Mphahlele's review in Lagos's *Service Magazine*) took over completely. *Poems from Black Africa,* the first major collection of its type, represents thirty-eight poets from eleven countries. Works by English-speaking Africans predominate, revealing mythic and mystical strains, grim superstitions. The African personality expresses itself in patterns: insistent references to toil, sexual exploitation by whites, ambiguous progress. Hughes's Biographical Notes and Foreword are informative. His well-chosen selections add modernity, delicacy, and beauty to the image of Africa.

In 1964, at his desk in "Harlem, U.S.A.," as his autographs style it, Hughes edited what amounts to "Poems from Black America." His *New Negro Poets: U.S.A.* averages two poems by each of thirty-seven postwar poets, a third of whom had already published volumes. The collection contains enough pieces praised in criticism here and abroad to augur a challenging future.[3] Hughes's contribution to the momentum of new creativity and to crystallizing literary theory among emerging Negro writers is implicit in Gwendolyn Brooks's Foreword. (Elaboration appears in "The Task of the Negro Writer as Artist" in *Negro Digest* for April, 1965, in which seven of these poets—and Hughes—speak out, and pronouncements of an equal number of them in *Sixes and Sevens* [1962], a London anthology.) Hughes's Biographical Notes add usable details.

In 1966, Hughes as editor still looked at two continents. His bilingual anthology, *La Poésie Négro-Américaine,* published then in Paris, enlarged the foreign reputations of Negro poets old and new. His collaboration with Arna Bontemps in updating their standard *The Poetry of the Negro, 1746-1949* will perform a like service in America.

V *"My world will not end."*

Only for a moment, while ending *I Wonder As I Wander,* does Hughes wonder whether his world will end. The durability of the world of his writings cannot be seriously questioned until its foundations in art have been seriously studied. Academic and professional critics—except for Negro scholars like Arna Bontemps, Arthur Davis, John Parker, Saunders Redding, and others

—have largely neglected him. No doctoral dissertation was devoted to his work before 1962. College anthologies have almost entirely excluded him. "Poetry as we know it," explains Karl Shapiro in *Book Week, New York Herald Tribune,* January 10, 1965, "remains the most lily-white of the arts."

1. *Reputation*

To assess Hughes's reputation one must turn away from the formal university community, which has viewed him superficially during his poetry readings. Aside from the few critics here and abroad who have grappled with his style and meaning, Hughes's reputation lies in the admiration of people the world over who buy his books and experience varieties of personal association with him. In the 1960's, his readers have seen him on television conducting tours of Harlem and explaining and introducing gospel music and jazz. They have heard him on radio, reading *Ask Your Mama* or talking about it with Irita Van Doren and John Kouwenhoven. And some were able to go with him to a "Twist Party" at Small's Paradise in Harlem to celebrate *Fight for Freedom.*

African readers have been able to personalize him in the 1960's: in Nigeria, attending the inauguration and, later, the festival on African and American Negro art; in Ghana, helping to dedicate an American library; in Uganda, speaking on "American Negro Writing." Students have found him easy to talk with, either in a crowded Parisian hotel or in a Harlem high school. His rapport with young people squares with a buoyancy in his writings that might partially account for the fact that students—at Wayne State, Fairleigh Dickinson, and Columbia Universities, to name three involved in the same year, 1963—are beginning to write essays and theses on him.

Of the approximately thirty-nine volumes of his own works published by 1967, twenty-seven are still in print, as are four of his collaborative books. Republications in English of his own volumes, and translations of them abroad, had appeared in the following genres at the start of the 1960's: the short story, the novel, the drama, the opera, the autobiography, the biography, and the miscellany of humor. His weekly column of mostly "Simple" pieces in the *New York Post* has enlivened readers to the scale of his interests: an eight-thousand-dollar bed in Ghana, a president "who came smiling out of the sky" into Dallas, and the bothersome memory of "my friend, Kurt Weill, whose music meant so much to the whole world, fleeing Berlin in the middle of the night because he was a Jew."

Hughes has faced the tests reserved for those who have something crucial to say. Picketed and demonstrated against by ultraconservative groups ranging from the Los Angeles YMCA faction in 1935 to Birchite pastors and "irate taxpayers" in Wichita in 1965, questioned about and cleared of alleged early Communist sympathies before the Senate Committee on Permanent Investigations in 1953, Hughes can still repeat a literal refrain in his poetry and prose: "I'm still here."

Talking about his renown abroad on January 29, 1965, he scored overseas American libraries for their sparse acquisitions of his and other Negroes' works. Despite this neglect, Hughes has long won the esteem of other countries, first on the Continent as a poet in the 1920's, later in Latin America, Asia, and Africa. His works now appear in several Indian dialects; and Simple, whose career is available to the French, Dutch, and Germans in the three-volume series, is the prototype for "Kugelfang," a beer-drinking German laborer created by the Berlin columnist Rudolf Reymer.[4]

2. *Poetry*

To sum up the lifework of a professional author is an impertinence minimized only by the concession that the lives of men are rarely judged by the average product or service which they exchange for daily bread. The fact that Hughes has written many verses of mere peppercorn for landladies and grocers fades behind the larger reality that he has created a score of poems worth the intimate study and respect of our best critical minds. Among his hundreds of poems written over a forty-five-year period, the following ten, ranked in their apparent order of excellence, are his best: "Mulatto," "The Negro Speaks of Rivers," "Song for a Dark Girl," "Jazzonia," "The Negro Mother," "Dream Variations," "The Breath of a Rose," "Minstrel Man," "Evenin' Air Blues," and "Dream Boogie." Below these, in a more readily debatable order, rank "Brass Spittoons," "The South," "To a Little Lover-Lass Dead," "Roland Hayes Beaten," "Judgment Day," "The Weary Blues," "Song for a Banjo Dance," "Negro Dancers," "Mother to Son," and "Southern Mammy Sings." These poems indicate the major stylistic and thematic emphases of Hughes: blues, jazz, be-bop and boogiewoogie; racial vehemence and romantic lyricism; Negritude and nonracial matter.

From a succession of lecture platforms and attic rooms, Hughes has freshened the current of American literature by ever experimenting and by ever spiralling through traditional forms. He has deepened that current, too, by coloring it zestfully and truthfully with many shades of Negro experience. Seeing life as a Negro so genuinely in his teens, he began his career with a vision and substance then in vogue. Broadening his experience through travel and social commerce in his twenties, largely among dark peoples and artists who accentuated his racial bent—though sometimes in that loneliness personally creative to him—he deepened his poetry with an ethnic passion not quite equalled in his later works. The fact that most of his best poems are early works shows an unlabored artistry able to mold beauty out of strong forces usually coalescent only in sentimental or exaggerated effusions.

Hughes, then, has recorded a poetic transcription of Negro folk life, with sensitive nonracial excursions. Although direct and clear (and sometimes sentimental) when traditional, he is stylistically most interesting when experimental. Through be-bop and folk slang, his "cool bop daddies," "aceboys," and women who "put de miz on" their men come alive. Night club names, newspaper headlines, visual patterns, and multiple protagonists shape or alter meanings. Plodding lines about nature, instructional and remonstrative verses about Negroes, and even intraracial scandal—according to some Negro critics—have come from Hughes. Yet, his quite typical "Dressed Up," in the same *Fine Clothes to the Jew* for which he was called a "sewer-dweller," has the straightforward charm and unplanned emotional appeal that predominate in his work. His best poems, and those numerous ones that faithfully portray the talk, moods, and habits of his urban folk, enrich our culture with a unique complex of truth.

3. *Fiction*

The exclusion of Hughes's stories from college anthologies and from the thorough attention of scholars is as indefensible as the exclusion of his poems. Written usually in comfort—in a warm hotel in Moscow, in a cottage at Carmel-by-the-Sea, in a genial flat in Mexico City, and at Hollow Hills Farm—his sixty-six published stories contain a dozen that merit critical examination: "Father and Son," "Little Dog," "Cora Unashamed," "Big Meeting," "On the Road," "On the Way Home," "The Blues I'm Playing," "A Good Job Gone," "Home," "Poor Little Black Fellow," "Professor," and "Slave on the Block."

A hundred and twelve reviews of the two volumes that contain forty-one stories represent available commentary. The variety, restraint, humor, naturalness, and power of the stories were commonly recognized; their pathos, irony, and realism less so; their tension, rhythm, imagery, and repartee barely at all. At least twenty-five Hughesian traits were overlooked, among them the linguistic play, lyrical exuberance, nonindividualized dialogue, and juxtapositions. Published observations of the stories are generally mediocre, sometimes observant, and here and there briefly penetrating.

The comprehensiveness and subtlety of the stories can be shown by a few partly statistical, partly analytical references to themes, images, and symbols. Selecting from the forty-odd themes, those found in more than ten percent of the stories, one can declare the author's overwhelming intention of revealing racial prejudice (thematic in thirty-eight stories) and, to a much lesser degree, of presenting usually delinquent fathers, affection-seeking women, interracial love, the cult of the Negro, religion and morality, the life of the artist, and jealousy. The images, classifiable into sixteen general types, cluster most vividly around nature, physical violence, and weariness. Half of the types represent rather uncomfortable stimuli, and half illuminate some fact about Negroes.

The symbolic substance of the narratives, delicately woven in seventeen varieties, is more imposing than the imagery and numerically more intense. Crosses, Negro voices and laughter, snow, coal, and steel are more suggestive than the flowers and springtime. The symbols, measured against Hughes's basically direct approach to material, are fairly rich. Conventional and contextual, they lace his stories with extra but uncontrived and unobscured meanings.

Not usually concerned with a complete rounding of his characters, the author intimately develops ten: Cora Jenkins, Mr. Lloyd, Oceola Jones, Clara Briggs, Colonel Norwood and Bert, Carl Anderson, Professor Brown, Charlie Lee, and Flora Belle

Yates (of "The Gun"). Yet, these portraits are not ideally full, for some details of appearance, activities, background, or range of emotion and attitude are missing.

Hughes's chief virtues as a writer of fiction—and more references to his two novels would not alter the conclusions—lie mostly in his style. The dialogue responds unerringly to facts of race. Hughes shapes its substance to the cadences, accents, and ductile phrases familiar to most Negroes; and he weaves incident, personality, and racial history into recurrent patterns. Interspersed songs feed into the stories a thumping rhythm that outlasts the passages admitting them. His Chekhovian endings, not an artifice of technique, are of a piece with the complexity of his themes, often leaving the reader nonplussed at the stubborn encounter between tradition and the individual.

Against the weaknesses of the stories (didacticism, nonindividualized dialogue—unseen "white folks" and voices talk—and many exclamations and parentheses) one might oppose two special distinctions in Hughes's personal and literary identities: his sympathy for human foibles and his honesty. A 1961 letter[5] by Hughes reveals both qualities:

> I feel as sorry for [whites] as I do for the Negroes usually involved in hurtful . . . situations. Through at least one (maybe *only* one) white character in each story, I try to indicate that "they are human, too." The young girl in CORA UNASHAMED, the artist in SLAVE ON THE BLOCK, the white woman in the red hat in HOME, the rich lover in A GOOD JOB GONE helping the boy through college, the sailor all shook up about his RED-HEADED BABY, the parents-by-adoption in POOR LITTLE BLACK FELLOW, the white kids in BERRY, the plantation owner in FATHER AND SON who wants to love his son, but there's the barrier of color between them. What I try to indicate is that circumstances and conditioning make it very hard for whites, in interracial relationships, each to his "own self to be true."

The honesty of heart and mind in part of the letter's page on "MYSELF IN MY STORIES" deserves also to be remembered:

> . . . I am most consciously in those based upon situations in which I have actually found myself in the past:
>   The object of over-much racial attention by white friends, . . . as in SLAVE ON THE BLOCK. I am in part Luther.

The object of interference by patronage with my objectives, as in THE BLUES I'M PLAYING. I am in part Oceola.

The son of a father who seemingly wanted to love—but it never happened—as in FATHER AND SON. I am Bert.

As a Negro American abroad, as in SOMETHING IN COMMON. I am Samuel Johnson.

As a Negro student in predominantly white schools prevented by color from achieving some of the things white students might achieve, as in ONE FRIDAY MORNING. I am Nancy Lee.

As one afraid to fully face realities, as the sailor of RED-HEADED BABY, the young man in ON THE WAY HOME or the father in BLESSED ASSURANCE. They are me.

.   .   .   .

Among my favorite characters . . . are Miss Pauline Jones in TAIN'T SO . . . and Sargeant in ON THE ROAD, probably because they are so completely self-contained—as I would like to be.

4. *Humor*

With humor, one of his rare gifts, Hughes injects comfortable chuckles into much of his poetry and prose. Often his humor has a cutting edge that pares down the social substance of horse-laughs and uproarious mirth—notably in the Simple books and columns—to a residual, mordant satire. It flexes in antic phrases, expressive of a creative joy linguistic in nature. In the mouths of Negro characters, that humor is often their way of transforming the ugliness in their environment. As the author's own interpretive style, it reveals a mind that steadily revolves the contradictions, the pretenses, and the bumptious weaknesses of mankind.

The best fruit of Hughes's humor is Jesse B. Semple, his one fully developed character, so real that, as "Simple," he has received mail addressed directly to him. Representative of the involvement of some readers in Simple's life is a Natchez, Mississippi, woman who, after seven years of sympathy for Joyce in her rivalry with Zarita, mailed her a Christmas gift in 1956: "a handsome handmade brassiere and panty set, with red bedroom slippers . . . in an embroidered silk bedroom bag" to enable her to "fight fire with fire."[6] It is also significant that Simple's sayings, rather like those of Benjamin Franklin's Poor Richard, have become proverbial in the pages of a calendar (issued since 1965 by New York's Carver Federal Savings and Loan Association).

5. *Theatrical and Musical Works*

Hughes's twenty-odd dramas, operas, musicals, and gospel song-plays, spanning thirty years, give body to his early expressed wish for a Negro national theater that would use authentic Negro material and be comparable perhaps to the Abbey Players. Disadvantaged by a commercial theater seldom interested in Negro drama, and therefore founding Negro theatrical groups in Los Angeles, Chicago, and Harlem along the way, Hughes has written tragedy, fantasy, and comedy. His plays about urban folk Negroes, best exemplified by *Simply Heavenly,* contribute to American folk drama the musical pulse and daily realities of a people not elsewhere accurately drawn by American playwrights.[7] His gospel song-plays are his liveliest fusion of music and drama, a combination that he has uniquely applied in his province.

6. *Nonfiction, Translations, and Editorial Work*

Since Hughes's first prose piece, "Mexican Games" (*Brownie's Book,* January, 1921), he has published many essays, autobiographies, biographies, histories, translations, and writings by other Negroes. The variety of his essays may be indicated by just a few titles: "Cowards from the Colleges," "Devils in Dixie and Naziland," "Fooling Our White Folks," "How to Be a Bad Writer," "Jokes Negroes Tell on Themselves," "People Without Shoes," and "Walt Whitman and the Negro." In *The Big Sea* and *I Wonder* he has written frankly and picturesquely of his experiences through 1937; and the sequel that he hopes to record should rival these works.

Hughes's biographical and historical nonfiction—seven of the eight volumes are juveniles—show his awareness of one of the most pressing needs of his times: the education of the young. He gives them the largely suppressed facts of Negro history to free them of blindness and prejudice. His translations of prose and poetry by dark-skinned Latin Americans also subserve this end. And his collaborative pictorial books document Negro history graphically.

Collaboration, mainly with Arna Bontemps, in poetry and in folklore advanced Hughes's editorial ambitions in the 1940's and 1950's. His work as editor in the 1960's widened to embrace

African and new Negro writers. Through influence on emerging writers in the New York area alone, and through the increasing attraction he presents as an editor to both domestic and foreign publishers, Hughes entrenches his position in a self-liberating American literature.

7. *The Poet Laureate*

As "the Poet Laureate of the Negro People," Hughes has earned the affection of black America. The admiration of dark peoples the world over is reflected in a proposal in the Caracas newspaper, *El Universal* (November 6, 1960), that Hughes be considered for the Nobel Prize. An intimate account of his reality is summed up in the many lines of poetry written to him or about him. His humanity mellows the stern comprehensiveness of the factual world he reveals; it reflects the whole man, native to a culture demanding of him emotional range and resiliency, fully responsive to the pressures uniquely felt by Negroes.

But Hughes's sympathy is firm. The end of the chapter on "Bricktop" in *The Big Sea* defines that firmness that shines in the fabric of his works. Bricktop Ada Smith, the freckled, likeable girl singer hastily summoned from Harlem to Paris in 1924 when Florence Embry quit the Grand Duc, began to cry when dawn found the club still empty on her opening night. Hughes, then a young dishwasher in the kitchen, tried to comfort her. But Bruce, the enormous one-eyed cook whose Cyclopian glare forever threatened invaders of the kitchen, turned to Bricktop and spoke prophetically and with unaccustomed gentleness the truth manifest in Hughes's works: "Life's a bitch—but you can beat it if you try."

Notes and References

Chapter One

1. For Hughes's account of his ancestry and earliest years, see *The Big Sea* (New York, 1940), pp. 11-21.

2. For biographical accounts and photographs, see Rose Leary Love, "The Five Brave Negroes with John Brown at Harpers Ferry," *The Negro History Bulletin*, XXVII (April, 1964), 164-69.

3. See *The New York Times*, Feb. 23, 1964.

4. See James A. Emanuel, "Langston Hughes' First Short Story: 'Mary Winosky,'" *Phylon*, XXII (Fall, 1961), 267-72.

5. See Emanuel, *The Short Stories of Langston Hughes* (unpublished Ph.D. dissertation, Columbia University, 1962), pp. 38-65.

6. See *The Big Sea*, pp. 223-55; Hugh M. Gloster, *Negro Voices in American Fiction* (Chapel Hill, North Carolina, 1948), pp. 101-15; John Hope Franklin, *From Slavery to Freedom* (New York, 1956), pp. 491-501.

7. *The Big Sea*, pp. 205, 217, 271-72.

8. Letter to Hughes from editor Donald Freeman, Jan. 19, 1926.

9. Quoted in Jones's review, *Chicago Defender*, Feb. 5, 1927.

10. Date calculable by use of *The Big Sea*, pp. 325, 331, and Hughes's *I Wonder As I Wander* (New York, 1956), pp. 3-4.

11. "The Dream Keeper" is listed in a 5x8 notebook in Hughes's files.

12. Hughes's agent until illness, about 1950, caused him to turn Hughes's affairs over to Ivan von Auw, Jr., of Harold Ober Associates.

13. Data from sheet found by Emanuel in unsorted materials in Hughes's basement, March, 1961, headed "FOR NOEL SULLIVAN:/ The First Drafts of my first short stories all written in 1933. Order in which they were written,/place, date, and periodical of publication" (hereafter called "Sullivan list").

14. Date of father's death calculable by use of *I Wonder*, pp. 285-87, and 3½x6 sheet headed "1934" in Hughes's files, giving dates thirteen works were mailed from Reno, San Francisco, and Carmel (hereafter called "1934 list").

15. See also Edward Lawson, "Theatre in a Suitcase," *Opportunity*, XLV (Dec., 1938), 360-61.

16. Interview with Hughes, Sept. 15, 1961; *Pittsburgh Courier*, April 15, 1939 (by-line Isabel M. Thompson); *Kansas City Call*, April 7, 1939. Emanuel's interviews (Sept. 15, 1960; July 17, 1961; Sept.

15, 1961; Nov. 13, 1961; Jan. 29, 1965), which are the sources of all of Hughes's oral statements except those on pp. 90, 92, 94, and 146, are hereafter noted and dated in the text.

17. *Chicago Bee*, Nov. 30, 1941, mentions his arrival; Chicago residence on his Feb., 1942, application for renewal of Rosenwald grant.

18. Hughes's July 26, 1964, postal card to Emanuel gives moving date as Jan. 1947; Mary Harrington's *New York Post* close-up, April 10, 1947, shows the St. Nicholas Avenue address.

19. Verse filed with Hughes's April 20, 1943, letter to Writers War Board. Other data come from 1942-43 correspondence with Board.

20. Spratlin's letter to Hughes, Nov. 5, 1951.

21. The James Weldon Johnson Memorial Collection at Yale University (hereafter called JWJMC) has story drafts notated with data used here.

Chapter Two

1. Sullivan list. It dates all stories discussed in this chapter.

2. Letter to Emanuel, July 5, 1961.

3. Letter to Hughes from Maxim Lieber, March 20, 1934; undated letter to Hughes from Lillian [May Ehrman] of Beverly Hills, California.

Chapter Three

1. Bradford A. Booth, "The Novel," *Contemporary Literary Scholarship: A Critical Review,* ed. Lewis Leary (New York, 1958), p. 263; Blyden Jackson, "The Negro's Image of the Universe as Reflected in His Fiction," *CLA Journal,* IV (Sept., 1960), 22-31.

2. *Monterey* (Calif.) *Peninsula Herald,* Dec. 12, 1958 (by-line Jack Benson).

3. Data from autographed drafts in JWJMC.

4. Sullivan list.

5. JWJMC, which has five drafts.

6. 1934 list; tear sheets of "Dr. Brown's Decision" in The Schomburg Collection, New York Public Library.

7. Hughes's list of forty-one stories, with partial publication data.

8. Copy of the illustrated story in Schomburg Collection.

9. JWJMC has two numbered and dated drafts.

10. Related Jan. 28, 1961, and quoted with Mr. Harper's permission.

11. Hughes's list of eleven stories on small sheet headed "OCTOBER 7, 1934."

12. "African Morning" and "Trouble with the Angels" are discussed in Emanuel, *The Short Stories,* pp. 152-54, 176-80.

Chapter Four

1. Script of interview on Dec. 10, quoted with permission of Division of Radio and Television, Protestant Episcopal Church, New York.

2. *Vancouver Sun,* Dec. 3, 1958.

3. *Michigan Chronicle,* May 8, 1943.

4. 1934 list; autographed and variously inscribed drafts mailed from Visalia, Calif., by Mrs. Josephine DeWitt Rhodehamel, Jan., 1961.

5. Two-page script, "Revised Version of Remarks by Langston Hughes Concerning Analysis of 'On the Road,'" dated June 16, 1957, received by Emanuel from Hughes in 1961 with note on reading at Kay Boyle's house.

6. Letter to Emanuel, July 5, 1961.

7. 1934 list shows ms. mailed from Reno, Oct. 29, at a time when dates of composition and mailing were habitually close.

8. 1934 list; *Esquire* tear sheets in Schomburg Collection.

9. *The Langston Hughes Reader* (New York, 1958), p. 483.

10. Letter to Maxim Lieber.

11. See Arthur P. Davis, "The Tragic Mulatto Theme in Six Works of Langston Hughes," *Phylon,* XVI (June, 1955), 195-204.

12. *Ibid.,* pp. 197-99, has a different interpretation.

13. 1934 list.

14. JWJMC has a copy of the note, signed by Hughes.

Chapter Five

1. See Davis's *Human Society* (New York, 1949), p. 386.

2. 1934 list.

3. *Idem.*

4. Drafts mailed to Emanuel in 1961 and 1962.

5. 1934 list.

6. *Idem.*

7. *Idem,* which also shows first draft of "Cora Unashamed" missing.

8. Letter to Hughes in Moscow from Blanche Knopf, May 8, 1933.

9. A note card on Hughes's folder of drafts shows six mailings, the first to *The New Yorker,* Oct. 31, 1941.

10. *Kansas City Call,* April 7, 1939.

11. 1934 list.

12. See, e.g., J. Saunders Redding in *New York Herald Tribune,* June 11, 1950; Kylie Tennant in *Sydney* (Australia) *Morning Herald,* May 15, 1954; Gilbert Millstein in *The New York Times Book Review,*

Sept. 29. 1957. Examples of corroborative letters in Hughes's files are his 1953 correspondence with Professors Irwin Edman of Columbia and Ben H. Lehman of the University of California.

13. See Emanuel, *The Short Stories*, pp. 250-64.

14. A pioneer exponent of Negro types and modern African patterns in art; one of the seven originators of *Fire*.

15. Hughes's file of "8 Short Stories . . ." shows this one mailed to *Orbit* (Montclair, N. J.), March 13, 1951.

Chapter Six

1. Lewis Nichols' interview, *The New York Times*, Oct. 27, 1963.

2. JWJMC has two folders with notes on projected African anthologies.

3. The review in *The Times Literary Supplement* (London), July 8, 1965, details both praise and challenge.

4. Letter from Reymer to Hughes, June 23, 1951.

5. Letter to Emanuel, Sept. 19, 1961 (containing permission to quote).

6. Ted Poston's close-up, *New York Post*, Nov. 24, 1957.

7. Webster Smalley's Introduction to his *Five Plays by Langston Hughes* (Bloomington, Indiana, 1963), p. xii.

Selected Bibliography

Only one full bibliography exists: Donald C. Dickinson, *A Bio-Bibliography of Langston Hughes, 1920-1965* (Hamden, Connecticut: Shoe String Press, 1967). Final sections in Therman B. O'Daniel, "A Langston Hughes Bibliography," *CLA Bulletin*, VII (1951), are informative. The following very selective list emphasizes the most useful and the most accessible of Hughes's works.

Much otherwise inaccessible material is in the James Weldon Johnson Memorial Collection at Yale University: letters to hundreds of correspondents; autographed revised drafts and typescripts of published and unpublished work; lecture notes; "Simple" columns; magazine and newspaper clippings; pamphlets and handbills, etc. Material of value is also in The Schomburg Collection in New York City and in Fisk University's Negroana Collection.

PRIMARY SOURCES

(*Listed Chronologically*)

A. Books

The Weary Blues. New York: Knopf, 1926.
Fine Clothes to the Jew. New York: Knopf, 1927.
Not Without Laughter. New York: Knopf, 1930.
Dear Lovely Death. Amenia, New York: Troutbeck Press, 1931. Privately printed.
The Dream Keeper. New York: Knopf, 1932.
The Ways of White Folks. New York: Knopf, 1934.
The Big Sea. New York: Knopf, 1940. Reprinted by Hill and Wang, New York, 1963.
Shakespeare in Harlem. New York: Knopf, 1942.
Masters of the Dew, by Jacques Roumain. Translated with Mercer Cook. New York: Reynal and Hitchcock, 1947.
Fields of Wonder. New York: Knopf, 1947.
Cuba Libre, by Nicolás Guillén. Translated with Ben Frederic Carruthers. Los Angeles: Ward Ritchie Press, 1948.
One-Way Ticket. New York: Knopf, 1949.
The Poetry of the Negro, 1746-1949. Co-editor with Arna Bontemps. Garden City: Doubleday, 1949.
Simple Speaks His Mind. New York: Simon and Schuster, 1950.
Montage of a Dream Deferred. New York: Henry Holt, 1951.
Romancero Gitano, by Federico García Lorca. Translated by Hughes. Published by *Beloit Poetry Journal,* 1951.
The First Book of Negroes. New York: Franklin Watts, 1952.

Selected Bibliography

Laughing to Keep from Crying. New York: Henry Holt, 1952.
Simple Takes a Wife. New York: Simon and Schuster, 1953.
Famous American Negroes. New York: Dodd, Mead, 1954.
The First Book of Rhythms. New York: Franklin Watts, 1954.
Famous Negro Music Makers. New York: Dodd, Mead, 1955.
The First Book of Jazz. New York: Franklin Watts, 1955.
The Sweet Flypaper of Life. Text by Hughes, photographs by Roy De Carava. New York: Simon and Schuster, 1955.
I Wonder As I Wander. New York: Rinehart, 1956. Reprinted by Hill and Wang, 1964.
The First Book of the West Indies. New York: Franklin Watts, 1956.
A Pictorial History of the Negro in America. Co-author with Milton Meltzer. New York: Crown Publishers, 1956.
Selected Poems of Gabriela Mistral. Translated by Hughes. Bloomington: Indiana University Press, 1957.
Simple Stakes a Claim. New York: Rinehart, 1957.
The Book of Negro Folklore. Co-editor with Arna Bontemps. New York: Dodd, Mead, 1958.
Famous Negro Heroes of America. New York: Dodd, Mead, 1958.
The Langston Hughes Reader. New York: George Braziller, 1958.
Selected Poems of Langston Hughes. New York: Knopf, 1959.
Tambourines to Glory. New York: John Day, 1959.
An African Treasury. Edited by Hughes. New York: Crown Publishers, 1960.
The First Book of Africa. New York: Franklin Watts, 1960.
Ask Your Mama. New York: Knopf, 1961.
The Best of Simple. New York: Hill and Wang, 1961.
Fight for Freedom: The Story of the NAACP. New York: Berkley, 1962.
Five Plays by Langston Hughes. Edited by Webster Smalley. Bloomington: Indiana University Press, 1963.
Poems from Black Africa. Edited by Hughes. Bloomington: Indiana University Press, 1963.
Something in Common and Other Stories. New York: Hill and Wang, 1963. Includes most of the stories in *Laughing to Keep from Crying;* adds one unpublished and eight uncollected stories.
New Negro Poets: U.S.A. Edited by Hughes. Bloomington: Indiana University Press, 1964.
Simple's Uncle Sam. New York: Hill and Wang, 1965.
The Book of Negro Humor. Edited by Hughes. New York: Dodd, Mead, 1966.
La Poésie Négro-Américaine. Edited by Hughes. Paris: Editions Seghers, 1966. Bilingual.
The Best Short Stories by Negro Writers. Edited by Hughes. Boston: Little, Brown, 1967.

Black Magic: A Pictorial History of the Negro in American Entertainment. Co-author with Milton Meltzer. Englewood Cliffs, New Jersey: Prentice-Hall, 1967.
The Panther and the Lash. New York: Knopf, 1967.

B. *Books with Introductions or Chapters by Hughes*

The Best of Negro Humor. JOHN H. JOHNSON and BEN BURNS, eds. Introduction by Hughes. Chicago: Negro Digest Publishing Co., 1945.
Primer for White Folks. BUCKLIN MOON, ed. "What Shall We Do About the South?" by Hughes. Garden City, New York: Doubleday, Doran, 1945.
TWAIN, MARK. *Pudd'nhead Wilson.* Introduction by Hughes. New York: Bantam Books, 1959.
The American Negro Writer and His Roots. "Writers: Black and White," by Hughes. New York: American Society of African Culture, 1960.
The Negro Since Emancipation. HARVEY WISH, ed. "My Early Days in Harlem," by Hughes. Englewood Cliffs, New Jersey: Prentice-Hall, 1964.

C. *Uncollected Pieces*

"The Negro Artist and the Racial Mountain," *The Nation,* CXXII (June 23, 1926), 692-94.
"Don't You Want to Be Free?," *One Act Play Magazine* (Oct. 1938), 359-93.
"Songs Called the Blues," *Phylon,* II (Summer, 1941), 143-45.
The "Simple" columns. *Chicago Defender,* 1943-1965.
"My Adventures as a Social Poet," *Phylon,* VIII (Fall, 1947), 205-12.
"Some Practical Observations: A Colloquy," *Phylon,* XI (Winter, 1950), 307-11.
"Langston Hughes on Writing," *Overview,* II (July, 1961), 38.
The "Simple" columns. *New York Post,* 1962-1965.
"Bread and Butter Side," *Saturday Review,* XLVI (April 20, 1963), 19-20.
"Hold Fast to Dreams," *Lincoln University Bulletin,* LXVII (July, 1964), 1-8.

D. *Interviews*

HARRINGTON, MARY. *New York Post* (April 10, 1947).
GIRSON, ROCHELLE. "This Week's Personality," *Saturday Review* (April 19, 1952).
MACGREGOR, MARTHA. *New York Post* (Sept. 15, 1957).
POSTON, TED. *New York Post* (Nov. 24, 1957).
Antioch College Record, XIV (Nov. 21, 1958).

Selected Bibliography

KENNEDY, DANA F. "Viewpoint" Series [scripts from broadcast tape
available], Division of Radio and Television, National Council
of the Protestant Episcopal Church, New York (Dec. 10, 1960).
POSTON, TED. *New York Post* (June 17, 1962).

SECONDARY SOURCES

A. *Books*

BARTON, REBECCA. *Witnesses for Freedom.* New York: Harper, 1948.
"The Big Sea" shows Hughes as a freedom-loving, freethinking
but race-conscious young writer.
BONE, ROBERT A. *The Negro Novel in America.* New Haven, Con-
necticut: Yale University Press, 1958. Useful comments on *Not
Without Laughter.*
EMANUEL, JAMES A. *The Short Stories of Langston Hughes.* Un-
published Ph.D. dissertation, Columbia University, 1962. Close
study of the short stories.
EMBREE, EDWIN. *13 Against the Odds.* New York: Viking, 1944.
"Shakespeare in Harlem" mixes biography with various personal
sketches.
GLOSTER, HUGH M. *Negro Voices in American Fiction.* Chapel Hill,
North Carolina: University of North Carolina Press, 1948. Com-
ments on *The Ways of White Folks* as emergent proletarianism
in Negro literature.
QUINOT, RAYMOND. *Langston Hughes, ou L'Étoile Noire.* Bruxelles:
Editions C.E.L.F., 1964. Combines historical and biographical
narrative with brief comments on twenty-odd poems.
REDDING, J. SAUNDERS. *To Make a Poet Black.* Chapel Hill: University
of North Carolina Press, 1939. Briefly contrasts emotional authen-
ticity and limitation of form in Hughes's first decade of work.
SMALLEY, WEBSTER (ed.). *Five Plays of Langston Hughes.* Blooming-
ton: Indiana University Press, 1963. Texts of "Mulatto," "Soul
Gone Home," "Little Ham," "Simply Heavenly," "Tambourines
to Glory." Smalley's Introduction surveys Hughes's pre-song-play
contributions in drama.
WAGNER, JEAN. *Les Poètes Nègres des États-Unis.* Paris: Librairie
Istra, 1963. Treats selected poems, and Hughes's role in Harlem
Renascence.

B. *Periodicals*

DAVIS, ARTHUR P. "The Harlem of Langston Hughes' Poetry," *Phylon,*
XIII (Winter, 1952), 276-83. Traces evolving thought in the
1926-1951 poems in its responses to an increasingly frustrated,
cynical Harlem.

————. "Jesse B. Semple: Negro American," *Phylon*, XV (Spring, 1954), 21-28. Examines Simple as a complex character and symbol of the urban Negro's tragedy.

————. "The Tragic Mulatto Theme in Six Works of Langston Hughes," *Phylon*, XVI (Winter, 1955), 195-204. Using "Cross," "Mulatto," "Father and Son," "African Morning," and *The Barrier*, Davis sees father-son conflict and parental rejection as Hughes's main concern.

EMANUEL, JAMES A. "Langston Hughes' First Short Story: 'Mary Winosky,'" *Phylon*, XXII (Fall, 1961), 267-72. Disclosure and discussion of story.

ISAACS, HAROLD. "Five Writers and Their African Ancestors," *Phylon*, XXI (Fall, 1960), 247-54. Conjectures about personal meaning of blackness and Africa to Hughes; sees him a unique explorer of ghetto life.

MACLEOD, NORMAN. "The Poetry and Argument of Langston Hughes," *The Crisis*, XLV (Nov., 1938), 358-59. Literary classification of *Don't You Want to Be Free?* and its reflection of conflicts in Hughes.

O'DANIEL, THERMAN B. "Lincoln's Man of Letters," *Lincoln University Bulletin*, LXVII (July, 1964), 9-12. Survey of Hughes's background and works.

PARKER, JOHN W. "Tomorrow in the Writing of Langston Hughes," *College English*, X (May, 1949), 438-41. References to poems of 1920's, 1930's, and 1940's tracing Hughes's thoughts as a "social poet."

PRESLEY, JAMES. "The American Dream of Langston Hughes," *Southwest Review*, XLVIII (Autumn, 1963), 380-86. Sees Hughes praised and attacked for this dominant theme; illustrated by references to several genres.

SPENCER, T. J. and CLARENCE RIVERS. "Langston Hughes: His Style and Optimism," *Drama Critique*, VII (Spring, 1964), 99-102. Useful for its excerpt from *Mule Bone* and for an approach not common in reviews.

WAGNER, JEAN. "Langston Hughes," *Information & Documents*, No. 135, Paris (Jan. 15, 1961), 30-35. Emphases, developed in his 1963 study, on Hughes's early life, broad attitudes, versatility, racial content.

Index